MW00674094

Sleep, Dream, Heal

Nocturnal Blessings to Help You Sleep,
Improve Your Health and
Discover the Wisdom of Your Dreams

Rev. Judith Christine Ternyik, M.A.

Published by ThunderHeart Publishing
P.O. Box 678
Sparta, NJ 07801

EDITORIAL OFFICE:
Blue Moon Wonders
4492 Camino De La Plaza
San Diego, CA 92173

Editorial and production: John Seeley, Bob Adams
Formatting by and typography: Sam Johnson
Cover design: Valorie Iglay, Leonardo, NJ
Cover Art by Katie Darvin, © 2016

Library of Congress Cataloguing-in-Publication Data
Ternyik, Judith Christine
Sleep Dream Heal / Judith Christine Ternyik
ISBN 0692696954 and the ISBN 13 is 9780692696958
Printed in the USA on acid-free paper
Distributed by Blue Moon Wonders

10 9 8 7 6 5 4 3 2 1

Manufactured in the United States

First Edition

Dedication

I dedicate this book "Sleep, Dream, Heal" to my mentor, teacher and best friend, John-Roger, even now in "Spirit," he is as close as my next breath. Thank you, J-R, for loving me more than I knew how to love myself.

Judith Ternyik

Acknowledgments

This book would have remained only a dream of mine without the coaching of John Seeley, who encouraged me throughout this process and got me "unstuck" to get my first book published. With John's expertise, patience and guidance I can now call myself a published author! I thank Teri Breier, who led me to John Seeley to take this into production and publication.

One of the first people who appreciated these dream blessings, which I posted on Facebook initially, was Allen Glasgow, along with Julia Snyder who both encouraged me to compile this collection of blessings into a book; thank you both for seeding the idea. With great appreciation for my very first "customer" who purchased my first book, I thank Siri Diane Welch, my Facebook friend for over seven years whom I finally met in person in the summer of 2015. We are kindred spirits for sure.

I'm grateful for all of you who whispered in my ear over the last few years how much these blessings supported you though challenging times; I'm thankful they made a difference for you. To all the gymnasts I have coached over the decades who have continued to ask me, "when is your book coming out?" And, "I want to read it," thank you all for your vision and planting the idea that I am an author. I thank another gymnastics friend, Marla Ranieri, who asked me a few years ago, "why don't you start writing books?" Thank you all for your encouragement and belief.

I am profoundly grateful to the talented Katie Darvin, for her amazing artistry in creating my book art, which she drew by hand! Katie spent many hours perfecting the artwork while balancing her gymnastics and high school studies!

With gratitude I acknowledge the amazing people who took time in their busy schedules to read my manuscript and write a recommendation: Dr. Steven Small, Sue Urda, Linda Nobel Topf, Jennifer Sweeton, Michael Stein and Eli Davidson, thank you all for your loving testimonials.

I am thankful for Valorie Iglay who came forward to complete the book cover. I appreciate her magical artistry with this beautiful cover and she also created my beautiful logo for ThunderHeart Publishing.

Vicki Ecker's final proofreading assisted in finalizing this manuscript to get it ready for press, of which I so appreciate her quick response and willingness to jump in at the final hours! I'm profoundly grateful for the time, effort and devotion of all who supported me in becoming a published author with "Sleep, Dream, Heal."

Table of Contents

"Judi's book offers tangible and easy steps to empower yourself with simple methods to attain a full night's rest. The collection of nightly dream blessings invites the reader to seek the light of spiritual wisdom through their dream journey. Connecting with our divine source each night is a blessing and 'Sleep, Dream, Heal' makes it easy to do."
Michael Stein, CEO of Genie Retail Energy and IDT Energy Network

"Sleep, Dream, Heal delivers exactly what the title promises—a heartfelt expression of Judi's own journey and the lessons she's learned along the way about sleeping well and dreaming each night that are crucial for our health and well-being. This book provides techniques to prepare you for obtaining a good solid night's sleep, while opening your inner wisdom through your dreams. This book is filled with sacred and divine expression that may lead your soul into new discoveries every night to Judi's own guiding question: 'In this moment, despite it all, who do I choose to be?'"
Linda Noble Topf- Author, "Wheelchair Wisdom: Awaken Your Spirit through Adversity"; "You Are Not Your Illness: Seven Principles for Meeting the Challenge"; 'Healthy Living' monthly columnist, <u>Huffington Post.</u>

"Read 'Sleep, Dream, Heal' each night to create within yourself a sense of peace, and to balance and integrate the functioning of your mind, body and soul. This book is infused with beautifully written, meditative nightly blessings and techniques that will help you to develop a deeper loving kindness, compassion, inner strength, emotion regulation, and self-awareness."
Jennifer Sweeton, Clinical Psychologist, Psy.D.

Sleep, Dream, Heal
Nocturnal Blessings to Help You Sleep, Improve Your Health and Discover the Wisdom of Your Dreams

Introduction

By: Reverend Judith Christine Ternyik, M.A

"The dream is an existential message. It is more than an unfinished situation; it is more than an unfulfilled wish; it is more than a prophecy. It is a message of yourself to yourself, to whatever part of you is listening. The dream is possibly the most spontaneous expression of the human being, a piece of art that we chisel out of our lives." ~**Frederick S. Perls**

"Sleep, Dream, Heal" offers you a quick and easy way to relax your body, release your thoughts and balance your emotions so you can induce a natural deep sleep throughout the night. The 13 categories of dream blessings will assist you in breathing and visualization techniques to allow your conscious mind to rest and invoke your subconscious mind to explore the dream realms.

You can choose a category like "Passion and Purpose" and read all 31 blessings for an entire month in one category. It takes about a full month to shift your awareness and begin new habits, and by focusing on one category per month you will invite the transformation process to unfold.

Many have eliminated their nightly nightmares by simply setting a "dream intention" by reading these powerful blessings each night.

The other option is to contemplate on your day and select a category that matches your experience, like "Stress Relief and Relaxation," or perhaps "Loss and Grief," and read one or two blessings to prepare your mind to receive what you need through your dreams. As you attain better sleep and are well rested you will enjoy a more balanced and productive day. The more you dream at night, the more mental and emotional freedom becomes available to you during your waking hours and the more your body will heal.

As you become more conscious of attaining a full night of well rested sleep, you may also begin to recall your dreams and open your consciousness more to exciting new vistas of discovering new aspects about yourself. That level of conscious awareness and "realization" will promote a deep integration of healing, balance and wellness towards attaining a state of homeostasis.

WHY SLEEP?

Every living thing sleeps… every living animal has a time to rest. Even the Bible talks about a time for everything under Heaven. Doctors induce a coma to help critically ill patients REST & HEAL while in a "sleep state," so the mind and emotions are still. When we are unable to get enough sleep our minds get fuzzy, our body aches and our emotions are more irritable.

—

Are you getting the sleep you need every night?

We require more sleep during different phases of our life. As infants and toddlers we sleep a lot, mostly because our brains are growing so rapidly that it's simply exhausting! Again as teenagers we need more sleep since our hormones are firing at rapid rates and huge growth spurts are underway. Stress affects people differently, as some will actually sleep much more during stress while others cannot sleep or rest at all!

Our daily life bombards us with over-stimulation through television, radio, city noise, people around us and our own inner self talk ...it's exhausting! Sometimes our bodies and brains are so revved up we cannot unwind and have the pendulum swing the other way to attain balance. Without balance we are due for a crash landing somewhere at some point.

Dysfunction sets in without ample rest. When we are sleep deprived our brains are altered, our body chemistry changes and we are on a path to create disease in our bodies.

LACK OF SLEEP = PUBLIC HEALTH EPIDEMIC

Sleep deprivation results in unhealthy behaviors like driving a car in a "trance-like" state, indulging in eating to comfort and calm our nerves and which may even shrink your brain!

What happens to you when you are overtired?

Your brain and body need to "night cycle" through deep sleep and dreaming. Just like a computer needs to be rebooted from time to time, our brains must reboot every night to remain optimally functional. It's not so much about how many hours you sleep; it's more about how many cycles your brain can complete and what your body needs to release and renew.

Reproducing cells and tissue is how the body cycles, and maintaining a consistent schedule of restful sleep will enhance your body's ability to renew itself.

Helpful ways to get a good night's sleep are: Take a shower or bath BEFORE bedtime to wash off the energy of the day; doing some passive stretching like Yoga or gentle dance movements will help to prepare and relax your body; light a candle as you prepare for bed but make sure you blow it out before drifting off to sleep; rub some scented oil on your neck and arms or spray some on your bed pillow. Lavender, Patchouli and Sandalwood work particularly well.

You can also create a pre-bedtime ritual by reading some spiritual or inspirational books or journaling, then taking time to meditate or listen to a visualization/relaxation CD. Find what works for you and create a loving, nurturing nightly ritual to enhance your sleeping habits.

WHY DREAM?

Both daydreams and dreams while sleeping provide rich value for our health and well-being. Dreaming offers an outlet for our subconscious minds to unload and download. The "dream process" also invigorates our creative imagination and problem solving abilities. Daydreaming gives us a "mini break" so our creative imagination can process or create while we "zone out" for awhile. It can induce relaxation and restoration for you and even more so if you journal what you "daydream" about. Attaining REM sleep, where your brain activity increases after resting during your sleep phase, is where dreams are made.

Dreams pave the way deep into our psyche and Spiritual dimensions within us. Dreams are one of the treasures inside each of us.

Throughout the history of mankind, several prominent leaders and Spiritual prophets have had clairvoyant premonition dreams as well as many inventors, philosophers, writers and healers who have been provoked and stimulated by a dream.

Are you aware of your dreams while sleeping?

Empirical data from studies of psychiatric patients indicate increased psychological imbalances when they're deprived of sleeping and dreaming. Dreams generate healing, balance and inspiration, which are all geared to invite us to tune into the wisdom within. When we are not able to connect with the "wisdom within" through meditation, prayer or dreams, our psyches are disturbed and can get very out of kilter.

The Meaning of Dreams

Dreams that are processing unresolved thoughts and feelings are simply unloading, completing and reorganizing to clear your channel and free up the mind and emotions. These types of dreams may not yield a meaning, for they are processing unconscious residue from your day and issues you're concerned about. These dreams are often weird, disconnected and seem nonsensical.

When you dream of a recurring event or similar symbols, that may indicate your subconscious mind is sending you a message. If a dream is haunting you daily because you keep thinking about it, or your dream lingers in your mind, then it's likely there is significant meaning for you to decipher. As you consistently jot down these dream fragments, over time a more conscious meaning may appear.

What images or feelings do you recall from your dreams?

Years ago I had a dream in which my subconscious was clearly sending me a message. My dream took place on a sunny beach by the ocean. Both my sisters and I were collecting seashells. My sister Marlene collected smaller clam shells. She said she could use them as ashtrays, nut and candy bowls.

As she piled them up on her beach towel, Janice, my other sister, was gathering really large clam shells. Janice wanted to paint them to use at her home as dinnerware, bird baths and unique sinks, and even create a waterfall in her flower garden with these huge shells.

As my sisters stayed on the dry, sandy beach collecting readily visible shells, I stood where the waves were crashing, where the water looked luminous and where I could see a very unique shell tumbling around just beyond my reach. Occasionally it would touch my leg but when I tried to grab it, the waves took it away. My sisters started hauling their collection off the beach as the sun began to set. But I walked further into the water seeking my unique shell.

Standing waist high in the crashing waves, I kept my focus on this very unique shell that had spirals of color and was as long as my arm. When I gave up catching it, I walked out of the water. Right then at my feet, in the foam of a gentle wave, my unique shell appeared, waiting for me to pick it up. As I lifted it out of the water and admired its beauty, the setting sun made this unique shell glisten with a rainbow of color. It may have once been a huge conch shell, but all that remained was the swirling center part. It made me think of a spiral staircase or DNA molecule. I carried my one and only unique shell to join my sisters with their own big shell collections.

When I awoke the next morning from my sleep I wrote this dream down in great detail. Over the next few days I was haunted by my dream and what the unique shell meant to me. What was the meaning for me, and why was my experience so very different from that of my sisters? What was I to do with this very unique shell?

What I gleaned was that Marlene was practical in collecting what she could immediately use. Janice wanted to create art and express beauty with her sea shells in her home. The spiral staircase DNA unique shell was a specific symbol for me. The meaning for me was, "as you create and begin anew, you will spiral upward in your consciousness and be shown great treasures to share with all."

Analyzing Dreams

I may have read every book ever written about dream analysis. As a university student, I took every class offered on dreams; "Interpersonal Communication in your Dreams, Jungian vs. Freudian Dream Analysis, Psychology behind Dreams," to name a few. I even began my Spiritual Journey through a class offered called "The Traveler in your Dreams," and so the topic of DREAMS lures me into learning more and more.

Since the age of 10, I've been so curious about dreams and have thirsted for knowledge on the subject. I read about various cultures that valued the dream process, such as the Egyptians, Hopi, Aborigine and many world and Spiritual leaders who had precognitive dreams. One of my favorite books was "The Prophet" by Kahlil Gibran, who also followed the wisdom he found in his dreams.

I have found that only YOU can ANALYZE and INTERPRET your OWN dreams. Though Jungian psychology has universal symbols and archetypal images for dreams for understanding meaning, I say it's the dreamer who must unravel and decipher meaning. Your own unique reference points are created throughout your life; even your siblings may relate differently to a dream symbol than you do.

What do you write in your dream journal daily?

One of my favorite techniques to analyze my dreams is using the Gestalt technique. You may also find the Jungian archetypal images of universal symbols helpful to get you started. Analyzing your own dreams is like discovering more of who you are deep down inside.

Gestalt is a process of revealing and peeling away the facade of your ego and personality to truly understand how you relate to people, situations and circumstances in your world.

Relationships and Dreams

Dreams can provide a plethora of information and "red flags," regarding, for instance, a relationship we may be considering becoming involved with or are already committed to. Whether this is with a significant other, a professional partner with a work related opportunity or a relocation to a new community, our dreams can often give us a heads-up in advance of the actual commitment.

It's truly remarkable what is available when we are aware and pay attention. Our Universe leaves clues all the time to provide us greater safety and success, but so many are unaware of the signs. Dreams are the most consistent and persistent signs telling us to simply pay attention.

Consider the ways your dreams may be warning you!

Years ago, I was offered a job which required relocation and initially being housed in the upper portion of the owners' home. Though they both were very gracious "courting" me to say yes and dangled many carrots to enhance the offer, I told them I'd have to sleep on it. THANK GOD I said that... for I did much more than sleep. Upon going to bed that night I reviewed my day, the interview, touring where I'd initially live ...and fell asleep. My dream played out a dramatic story for me.

In my dream I had accepted the offer and moved into the upper apartment above their home. After a few weeks, things turned very sour very quickly... the wife turned into a witch, a very wicked witch with green skin and all. The husband turned into a devil complete with horns and a long tail! They kept me living above them as a prisoner and made it so I'd never be able to escape. I had to work for them forever without freedom. THEN I WOKE UP in a sweat! I called them up and declined their offer. Wow, thank God for my dream.

When you learn your own personal "dream symbols," deciphering your dreams will become faster and easier. When I dream of a dog it means that I'm dreaming about a man, a significant male in my life. I learned this after applying a Gestalt technique on a bizarre recurring dream theme I had, but with different dogs and scenarios. Three short dreams in one week gave me the answers I sought.

What gems are in your dreams that offer great wisdom for you?

Dream 1: I'm at a hotel ready to judge a gymnastics meet and I'm putting on my pantyhose. I walk out of the hotel door and a little Chihuahua dog comes running down the hall and nips at my ankles and runs my stockings. I have to go back into my room and change my pantyhose; this happened three times all in a row with the same dog. (From that dream on I always carried extra pantyhose when I traveled to judge meets.)

Dream 2: I'm in my small house ironing when I get a call from Danskin in NYC (I was actually consulting with them at that time) and had to quickly get ready, for they had a plane ticket for me to travel. I put on a beautiful outfit to travel in and quickly packed a bag. As I was leaving a Dachshund came running at me then started to fly with his ears. He was flying circles around me keeping me from walking out the door to take my trip. It was like a large mosquito chasing me but it was a flying dog! I finally got out the door and ran to get my car.

Dream 3: I'm preparing to attend an event hosted by Insight Seminars (Personal/Spiritual growth training which I actually did attend at the time) and after I left my house and was walking to my car a small Poodle dog darts out of the garden and starts nipping at my feet and barking loud keeping me from getting into my car.

TIME TO ANALYZE THIS: I used a Gestalt technique where I set up two chairs. I sat in one chair and asked the question to each separate dog. Then I sat in the "dog chair" and answered that question. It helps to get out of your mind and into a receptive state almost like an altered consciousness for this process to flow easily. The bottom line was that each dog was actually my live-in boyfriend at the time! He (the dream dog) did not want me to venture out into life and possibly drift away from him. He (the dream dog) wanted me to stay home cooking, ironing, typing his papers, cleaning and also continue with my formal education. He (the dream dog) was frightened and threatened that I was growing, and evolving into several different areas that he himself was unwilling to approach.

How do you reflect on the meaning of your dreams?

After that dream, I reflected on our 5-year relationship... the good, the bad and the ugly. It was clear that I found it unacceptable to stay with a man who felt he had to limit me because he did not want to venture out and grow or develop more. We dissolved our relationship both personally and professionally and went our separate ways. I never ever again had a dream of a small, well-groomed dog nipping at my ankles or spinning circles around me to keep me put.

However, WHY A DOG? I leaned that for me Dogs=Men in my dreams. Now, I'm a huge dog lover, I have dogs, rescue and foster dogs... I'm like the dog whisperer in real life. But after dreaming of a big, dirty, unkempt street dog I had to know why. At the time I was dating someone whom I thought was "it" for me. But my dreams were indicating otherwise.

After much introspection about why my dream dog represents a significant male, I got my answer. When I was very young we had a Collie named Ginger. She was older and I was about four. I loved her so much, we did everything together and she even let me boss her around (I was a very bossy little girl). Then came the day Ginger died due to old age and a rare skin disorder ...I cried my eyes out from the ages of five to nine. Four years of crying because I missed her so much. EUREKA! Other than my Mother and Father my first real love was GINGER, a dog. This is why I think that my "dream dogs" represent men I have loved... it makes sense to me.

If you have a relationship issue, or perhaps you yearn to attract a relationship to you... simply write it down in your journal before you go to bed. You will then "program your dream state" to provide avenues for you to pursue in resolving or attracting what you desire. The process can be very revealing, exciting and sometimes life changing. Reading a blessing to help your body, mind and emotions to relax so you will become more receptive to your dreams is a good practice. Create an enjoyable ritual before bedtime or meditation time... nurture yourself, prepare with reverence and look forward to your dreams. Your dreams can take you where your mind cannot.

Set your nightly intention to "program your dream channel"
to work out the issues and concerns you have!

Both Sleeping and Dreaming Are Healing

Your sleep time tonight, is not just for your physical body to rest and recuperate... it is also for your DREAM-TIME where your mind and emotions can download and process events. Night travel opens the gateway for Soul Travel to traverse the realms of Spirit. Appreciate the opportunity and possibilities you have each night to heal, align and discover as you rest, for when you rest you're becoming your best!

Be a neutral observer of your dreams whether they be night mares or intense or even very pleasant. You are totally safe within each dream so simply relax and surrender to your own inner adventure. It's helpful to write down your dreams or symbols/images each time you awaken as that will increase your conscious awareness of the value in each dream.

Take in a deep breath and know that every experience is for your evolution and transformation. Let the sleep begin, bring on the dreams and let's all heal together during our night journey traveling through our dreams.

SWEET DREAMS!

Judith Ternyik

Abundance & Prosperity

Open your hearts and your mind to receive! Be willing to let go of what you no longer need, use or want and make room for Prosperity and Abundance to enter your life. De-clutter your thoughts and feelings as well as your living space also and create open flow because the universe will fill a void.

These dream blessings focus on clearing the blocks you may have to attract more prosperity into your life and to generate abundance for yourself. As we fall asleep with a prayer and intention our dreams often will provide keen insight regarding what we deserve to enjoy more of in our lives. Pay attention to the shift in your awareness as your dreams leave clues for you to follow in your waking life. Everyone deserves to live a prosperous life filled with abundance.

"There is something you must always remember. You are braver than you believe, stronger than you seem, and smarter than you think." ~ **Winnie the Pooh**

♥Share your gratitudes as you acknowledge your blessings. From your peaceful center of abundance, stream into your dreams and travel with your Soul towards new vistas and discoveries. You renew yourself with every breath so renew yourself every night with every dream and "ah ha" moments to render yourself to endless blessings. Your gratitude will open the flood gates to receive greater abundance and riches... dream sweetly!

♥YOU are worthy so ask for what you want, desire and deserve to experience, have and enjoy. Invite your dreams to provide keys and the pathway towards manifesting a transformation. Feel the healing throughout your body, ride the energy of your dreams into the Beloved Spirit and reconnect with who you are. It's in the realization that we become real and acknowledge our worthiness, and then we are open to receive the abundance.

♥Breathe in the LIGHT, and RELAX into the night, follow your DREAMS into deeper realms of reality that your conscious mind may not relate to. TRUST your process and allow the blessings to anoint you with treasures beyond your imagination. YOUR LIFE IS FOR YOU, and nothing is against you. Keep moving TOWARDS what you DESERVE to ENJOY on all levels of your Soul and this life you now live. Invite the LIGHT to expand you and transform you. LOVE is generous, LOVE is gentle and kind, LOVE is who you are! Embrace the pure essence of your loving light and transform yourself tonight with every breath to receive and prosper.

♥Opening is expansion, growing, thriving and evolving. Like a parachute, the mind works best when it's open. Let's ALL OPEN to the POSSIBILITIES available to us through Spirits divine intervention and the grace of God. What if all that we dream, desire and deserve are all WITHIN REACH but we are contracted and closed to receive it? OPEN, LET GO, RELAX, RELEASE, SURRENDER and... receive what is there for you, waiting for you, within reach. May you be embraced by the rapture of Spirit, Light and all that is holy and sacred. Blessings, to you, for a wonderful restful sleep, and a renewal for your whole life. Abundance is yours to enjoy so simply claim it.

♥Release your worries and concerns over money on this worldly level tonight. Send it all up to the divine light within you tonight. Move into a deep sleep and invite your dreams to guide you into the answers and resolutions which you seek in your life. Put your subconscious mind and intuitive psyche to generate ways to succeed in the path to health, wealth, riches and abundance, for you were not created to be in poverty or lack. Spark your creative imagination and let each dream leave you a clue with your next steps and ride your dreams into the greater knowing within yourself.

♥Simply let the past fall away as you bless yourself tonight and fall asleep. Drift into your dreams and even past your dreams to new discoveries within your consciousness. Explore more and renew yourself so the veil of Light and Spirit will soothe you tonight as you open yourself in wonderful ways to receive and enjoy. Affirm your worthiness to live a rich and abundant life and believe you deserve to receive the very best in your life. Now breathe into that open space and receive your dreams.

♥Escape this world tonight and enter the dream world as your body restores through a healing restful sleep. Your Soul and your subconscious will travel into the inner realms of worlds without end, into the vistas of awareness to open your abundance consciousness. Explore it all in your body of light all through the night and engage in esoteric understanding beyond this reality. Ignite your spirit and spark your Soul... quite your mind and surrender it all to receive the best possible.

♥Sweet nocturnal blessings to all tonight as you review your day and acknowledge what you're grateful for. Doing this before you rest will fill your heart with a peaceful joy. Expansion of abundance and goodness can be very healing on your body and may soothe your Soul too. Ask for greater awareness in your dreams to gain more insight about answers or direction that you may be seeking. An attitude of gratitude opens up the space to receive and prosper.

♥With each breath that you take, bring healing light to yourself tonight. Let your mind wander through the wonder of your sacred dreams this evening. Allow your energy to blossom and traverse the worlds without end to flourish in the fertile fields of possibilities, riches and abundance. Notice everything. Pay attention for there are many "ah ha's" for you to take with you; and transform your waking state into a plethora of prosperity, now take in a deep breath and receive as you affirm your worthiness of receiving the blessings.

♥Put your heart at ease and your mind at rest, so you can dream your very best. Take in a pure full breath and fill your body with nourishment as you put this day behind you and journey into your dreams. Make a request for clarity, direction or healing though your nightly Soul Travel ...and drift deeply into an altered state. Be open to receive the treasures of prosperity and abundance that are yours to claim. Be aware of the images that you see, hear and feel; as you traverse the inner realms for they serve as keys for your next step. Let your dreams be your guide.

♥Embrace the night, embrace yourself and drift off to sleep... deeply and gently. Let the light engulf you as you enter the realms of worlds without end where the past falls away and you are totally present. Keep radiating your own light beyond the shadows through the darkness, doubt, fear and shame to illuminate as far as your energy will extend. The more your give the greater you will receive so start by giving to yourself all the love, abundance, prosperity and joy you desire. Enjoy your dreams with all of your senses engaged and expand your consciousness into the sacred energies of living love with gratitude for the abundance you have and the prosperity ahead.

♥Give your worries and concerns over to the divine light within you tonight. Empty out what no longer serves you to make space to receive and attract the abundance you deserve. While you rest and sleep let your dreams soar to realms within realms and create the possibilities for you to succeed, prosper and flourish. Breathe deeply and melt into the sacred space for your Soul to remember itself to all that is, which is pure and sacred. You are already perfect. You're in the process of remembering that. OPEN TO THE POSSIBILITIES of wealth for yourself in all ways wonderful!

♥Allow the night to take you deeply into your dreams as you surrender this day and what blocks you from abundance. Simply breathe and release your tension so your body will restore, relax and heal... as your inner light ascends into your tunnel of dreams where riches await your arrival. Gather the wisdom that each dream offers and take this awareness into your next day and watch the abundance appear. The more you let go the more you receive so renew yourself tonight within each dream.

♥Kick back and gaze into the night sky... breathe in the cool fresh air and let it expand into your body and imagination into a state of receptivity. Prepare for a dreamy night to collect the pieces of gems that you'll recall when you're awake ...sleep deeply so your physical body can rest and recover and your imagination will be seeded with a consciousness of wealth. Ride the energy of your dream stream until your Soul is nourished with the sacred travels through the sound and light of Spirit. Keep your heart open, loving and flowing and your Spiritual awakening will continue ongoing. Claim the wealth and prosperity waiting for you to receive it.

♥Ascend tonight as you fall into slumber lift higher to travel the inner levels of Light and Sound. There is much to learn and more to know as you release this level, and begin to let go. Let the past fall away to receive the consciousness of "now." You may see silhouettes of light and shapes of colors that continue to shift and change as you travel deeper through the inner realms as each glimpse offers you a key to attaining the prosperity you deserve. Profound awareness awaits your awakening, goodness and God-ness are yours to behold. Dream deeply, sweetly and gently tonight as you open more to receive and prosper in every way.

♥Wrap yourself in a cocoon of purple light and extend this hue of radiant energy beyond your body to envelop our whole planet too. Breathe in the calm and be present in this moment as you surrender and enter the dream portal. Bask in the treasures that are waiting for you in your night travels through this journey with your dreams see yourself partaking in the abundance and prosperity that is already yours to claim. Align yourself with the presence of Spirit as you experience your own divinity and worthiness to receive your blessings. Bask in the light of divine perfection and receive the treasures that are already yours.

♥Invite your Soul into your dreams and be open to everything. Let yourself "image in" and imagine what may seem impossible now and claim your worth. Your clear intention to delve into deeper levels of consciousness and wisdom will open the flood gates of your dream world. Let go as your Soul travels beyond the mystery schools into worlds without end, where you will receive the keys to unlock the treasures of wealth. Every glimmer and glimpse is for your awakening... just put the puzzle together. Take the leap of faith and dive into your dreams into the treasure chest of abundance and prosperity.

♥Take some time to express gratitude and count your blessings as you observe the energetic shift in energy around you. Anoint yourself with goodness as you let your body go into deep relaxation and total rest. BREATHE DEEPLY of the peace that is present and envelop yourself with divine light as you drift off into your dreams into a state of receptivity and calm. Let your dreams lead you into places where your conscious mind cannot go and marvel at the magnificent wisdom and abundance being shown to you and give thanks as you prosper.

♥Release your concerns and prepare for a restful sleep... let go and flow with the energy of grace and be thankful for what you have in your life now. Let your loving heart anoint you with goodness and healing renewal as you nurture yourself with affirmations of abundance. As you soothe and energize your body, you will begin your dream world with open receptivity to the inner realms of prosperity. Clear your channel and be open to receive the blessings for each dream holds keys to your freedom for you to enjoy a full life of generous abundance and prosperity.

♥Find your sacred center, your inner sanctuary and take refuge there. Breathe deeply of the peaceful calm from the center of your being and release all the things of this world. Bathe yourself in divine light and anoint your body with healing and an openness to receive the ease and grace you deserve to have. Hush the sounds around you, calm the fears that haunt you to hear the sound current within you and follow that sacred lullaby into your dreams. Explore your dreams with wonder and awe as you gather the gems of wisdom and treasures within each one. Surround yourself with the riches you find within your Soul.

♥Dream time is luring you into a deeply relaxing and healing sleep. It's time to alter your state of consciousness and turn inward to the other levels of being that you also are. Let go of any fear of "poverty consciousness" and affirm that you are richer than you realize. Surrender this day and embrace the night as you transform into your dream threads weaving a tapestry of mystical wonder. Every dream has a message for you, use your keen awareness to sense each gem and find the blessing within each gem. You are a treasure chest waiting to be discovered so open up to receive the abundance within you for prosperity is your divine right.

♥Time to take in a deep breath into the center of your heart and let it expand into your loving focus of peace... exhale the frazzled chaos of the day and breathe in calm. Time to let your dreams lead the way to solutions, riches and journeys, for your Soul to enjoy and your wealth consciousness to awaken to. Become like the breath that you breathe... formless, light, expansive and follow your dreams into the through the worlds without end. Breathe deeply from this expansive state of being and receive the wealth you deserve to enjoy and live a prosperous life.

8

♥Nighty-night is the perfect time to delve deeply into the myriad dreams tonight and update your belief system. Become the neutral observer as you watch and listen for each dream and symbol that unfolds for you, to attract greater wealth, abundance and prosperity into your life. Ask why you suffer a life of lack; and if you are blocking from receiving the abundance you deserve? The treasure chest of riches is within you; simply be open to receive and allow them to transform your life into health, wealth and happiness. Awaken with a consciousness of prosperity!

♥Release all that distracts you from your essence, your inner light, your true self, which includes any fears of creating and having the abundance you desire. Breathe deeply of the dream vapors which lure you into sleep and Soul travel through the night. Engage yourself in a wondrous discovery into the most sacred esoteric realms deep within your consciousness; where it is waiting for you to acknowledge and affirm your prosperity and wealth. Simply keep moving your awareness further... for there is always more and you deserve the very best.

♥Emerge tonight into the greatness that you are; and embrace the fullness of the light as you expand your consciousness into your dream vortex. Receive what is waiting for you to partake in the riches and abundance that have been preordained. Keep opening your senses to fully explore the wisdom unfolding for you; and bringing comfort and ease into your life. Every dream offers a key to greater knowledge, wisdom and abundance so dream the night away and enjoy your journey as you transform into greatness as you acknowledge your worthiness to receive the wealth you deserve.

♥May each of us make a Holy Shift tonight in our sleep, our meditation and in our dreams. Let's all awake in the morning with an awakening of consciousness to the abundant prosperity ordained for us all. Ponder what's on the other side waiting for you... then enter your dreams tonight with anticipation and wonder. You can AWAKEN during your night time dreams..."lucid dreams" can show you how you can consciously be in more than one place at the same time. Happy Dreaming... may we all awaken to the abundance waiting for us for it is within your grasp.

♥Tonight as you prepare for sleep, leave your body behind when you reach out beyond your boundaries. Clear your mind and calm your emotions as you extend your energy, your essence directly towards your dream stream and into the prosperity waiting for you. Send your blessings to all that you see and become aware of as you dream travel tonight for the more grateful you are for what you have the more you will attract the abundance you deserve to enjoy. Keep blessing it all like an ongoing mantra. Allow this blessing to envelop you for YOU ARE THE BLESSING! You are wealthy with riches.

♥Lay down tonight as if you're floating in water, back in the womb... safe, trusting, surrounded and embraced in the element we were created in. Let your body expand, stretch, open and become weightless as it relaxes fully into the nighttime sleep journey. Lift your Spirit into the light above your physical body keep elevating your consciousness higher until it floats effortlessly into the brilliance of your Soul Body. From this lighter state of being simply float like air into other dream vortexes and states of being, knowing that you are already rich and prosperous with overflowing abundance. You are a magnificent being of pure divine light... delight in that. Awaken with a mindset of wealth and create your life.

♥BREATHE DEEPLY and RELAX INTO THE DARK of the night, let your body melt into your bed and fall asleep. Give your imagination permission to wander into the dream field of abundance and riches; as you take a trip beyond reality into the vast prosperity of wealth waiting to be discovered. Notice the shapes and colors during your journey inward and outwardly, into realms of other realities. Use everything to your advancement and learn, grow and be in the know. Relish in the brilliant beauty that is here for you. You are all of this and much more in your treasure chest of resources and wealth.

♥Melt your worries, concerns and fear of lack tonight and merge into the light as you release into your peaceful slumber. Ascend into your dream vortex and let the process of receiving a life of prosperity unfold in perfect images, symbols all in full color. Take in the creative splendor of your dream realm and know that all goodness is being prepared for you as you open to the abundance waiting for you to claim. Just breathe, receive and bless each moment for dreams do come true.

♥BE NEW tonight and imagine the life you deserve right here and now! Take the time to BREATHE and relax into your restful sleep tonight and invite your DREAMS to transport you into amazing spaces and places of wonder and discovery. The more you LET GO the more space you create for your own RENEWAL. Dream of the life you are ready to receive and awaken to taking action steps towards your dream life.

"Silence is the sleep that nourishes wisdom." ~ **Francis Bacon**

Judith Ternyik

Breath & Essence

Breathing is a key to focus your intention, purpose and you're Soul. We may not see the air we breathe but we still keep breathing it; for it sustains our life. Many cultures have practiced conscious breathing as a way of preparing for an event and you can use it to prepare for a deep sleep.

The quality of essence is beyond the physical level, it is a nuance, a glint as an energy or feeling that can elevate your consciousness and awareness toward the Spiritual and Soul realms. When you experience your essence, it is beyond peaceful. You may feel a stillness; all thoughts and feelings will cease; yet you will be more keenly focused and aware of the present moment than ever before. Each dream blessing offers a key to moving beyond this physical form and this Earth level so you can ascend into your dreams with lightness and ease.

"Empty yourself of everything. Let the mind rest at peace. The ten thousand things rise and fall while the Self watches their return. They grow and flourish and then return to the source. Returning to the source is stillness, which is the way of nature." ~ **LAO TZU**

♥Tonight... escape your body and this physical world by BREATHING in the sacred divine light... and take off! Enter into a space, a place where you know all is perfect, calm and peaceful. This is your source, the center of being, your very essence. From this stillness expand into your dream state. Enter into the misty veil of your dreams through the inner worlds without end, as you travel in your Soul to the mystery schools of ancient knowledge. Explore what is present for you to discover and devour the blessings with rapture and gratitude, and inhale the goodness.

♥Now take in a deep full expansive breath, and exhale with a sacred sound. The song of the Divine is always present within you. Listen for the harmony and healing vibration as you gently fall asleep. Listen for your inner song and let the music move you and harmonize with others of the same resonating sound. Rest well and restore yourself with each and every dream.

♥Nurture yourself with deep breaths and with every exhale express what you're grateful for... keep going until you feel the light moving through you. Receive the sacred blessings of the moon and the stars this night while you float into your dream state. Focus on your breath, your heart center and the light that you are. Every dream reveals a piece of your life, pay attention and keep breathing, keep dreaming.

♥Breathe in deeply and release with a sigh ...ahh... Relax into your sleep and invite your body to restore and heal on all levels. Ascend into your light and float into your essence as you begin your dream journey tonight. Be here and there and aware of it all through your lucid dreaming and Soul travel. On the other side of each dream is your dream come true.

♥Indulge in the quiet of the night; where you can take in a deep breath and sigh gently to hush your mind. Reflect on nothing and let yourself unwind, relax and receive. When sleep overcomes you, release into your dreams with ease and grace to the possibilities available to you. Melt into each dream, became aware of the essence which you are and embrace every symbol as you transform your awareness in every way.

♥Time to take in a deep breath into the center of your heart and let it expand into your loving focus of peace... exhale the frazzled chaos of the day and breathe in calm. Time to let your dreams lead the way to solutions, and journeys for your Soul to enjoy, and your consciousness to awaken to. Become like the breath that you breathe ...formless, light, expansive and follow your dreams into the path through the worlds without end. Breathe deeply from this expansive state of being, which is your true essence.

♥Gently breathe in deeply and expand your lungs completely then expand your body fully and as you release that breath let everything totally empty from your thoughts and feelings. Breathe gently as you send healing light to your physical body and settle down for a long restful sleep. Feel the vibration of light tingle on your skin as you transform into the essence of energy and melt into your dreams. Observe your dreams and gather the gems of wisdom for you to remember long after the dream is over. Awake each morning a "new you" with more dream gems to apply to your life.

♥Breathe so fully your cells separate, your body expands into a deep relaxation and has space to heal. Breathe so deeply that your heart is breathing you. Breathe beyond your physical body and open up to enter your dream vortex. Float on the Ether of light into mystical esoteric realms of wonder and awe, as you travel beyond your dreams. It's time to Soul travel so take a deep breath and go... and keep breathing.

♥Receive your breath deeply, and hold it until you feel expansion in your body. Then release your breath as you release the day fully and completely. Breathe in the peace of the night and let your body sink deeply and melt into a puddle of relaxation. Ascend from your body into the light and place your attention on the essence, not the form. Breathe into your dreams so they transport you into the esoteric mystical realms of Soul awareness, and transcend this level. Let your dreams and loving lead the way.

♥Inhale a deep breath and sustain it through your body. As you exhale, let everything leave your body that is not in balance with divine perfection. Take in a gentle breath and invite your dreams to usher in; and take you into the deeper levels of your being directly to the core of your essence. Transform yourself into every possibility which will seed to your health, wealth and balance. Delve deeply into each dream. The more open you are and less attached to what should be, the more gifts you can receive though the magic of the night and the mystery of your dreams.

♥Allow a deep breath through the center of your heart and expand that fullness throughout your body ...relax as you empty your breath. Welcome your restful slumber with lucid dreams that offer gems of awakening and awareness for you. Traverse the realms of light with wonder and grace as each dream weaves your tapestry. Float gently towards your dreamscape with wonder, grace and ease as you rise and fall with each sacred breath.

♥Sink gracefully into your physical body during your slumber tonight. Exhale slowly so you can lift your body of light into the highest place you can ascend to, right into the essence of your being. When you reach the point of suspension, quiet, simple delicate joy... breathe it in fully and allow that to transform you on every level. Hover and sustain yourself within the peace of your Soul; as you travel through your dream voyages and discover what truly is authentic for you.

♥Take pause to simply breathe deeply and sustain your breath. Fill yourself with life, flood yourself with light. Energize and heal every cell in your body through breathing the sacred breath. Surrender your attachments to this world to gracefully enter other worlds. Within the essence that you are, travel into the endless worlds without end, where your dreams will escort you within your consciousness via your dream portal.

♥Peace is present... just be still and listen for the sound of peace. Breathe it in. This worldly level can be so very challenging. Perhaps a reminder that it a temporary place for us all. Bring your awareness into the light of your spirit, until you touch the essence of your Soul. Breathe deeply and fully from that sacred center as you begin your night journey of dream travels with each breath. Follow your dreams as they reveal what cannot be seen with your eyes.

♥Inhale all the blessings you can imagine as you breathe deeply and sustain your life. Exhale all the past and concerns you may have... be present here and now. Fall asleep with a sense of adventure as you jettison yourself into your dream journey, into the inner cosmos. Embrace the light and let it illuminate your way as you deepen your awareness in your conscious awakening. Gather the gifts your Soul travels avail to you this night, and create an amazing life for yourself with them.

♥Release and relax your body with each deep breath to allow your surrender to your slumber. Take a peek through your dreams to the inner realms within you. Dream lucid dreams tonight, and surrender what you think you know to discover deeper truths your essence knows. Listen for the sounds as you are guided by the light into deeper levels of consciousness. Sometimes we can awaken when we fall asleep, just keep breathing in and out and dream the night away.

♥Breathe yourself into your dreams... rest your body and ascend into the dream realms tonight. Float, drift, glide and tumble your way through multi levels of consciousness; while you enjoy the adventure of this inner dream journey. Keep moving, traveling, learning and awaken to the mystical esoteric knowledge your dreams may offer to you. Everything is FOR YOU so receive with joy and gratitude.

♥Close your eyes and open your imagination as you fall asleep tonight. Breathe deeply of the peaceful calm that is present for you to receive. Drift into your dreams with gentle flow and graceful ease as your breath dances on your lips. Dance on the wings of your dreams all night through and discover the mystical mysteries that are waiting for you deep within the essence of your being.

♥Invite your dreams take you into the night so relax deeply and breathe fully as you drift off to sleep. Follow your stream of dreams through all the adventures on the inner levels. Soul travel into the highest light as you surrender the day to gain perspective and insight. Your true essence knows what your mind yearns to learn. Dream sweetly and rest well as you let your breath rise and fall with deeper relaxation.

♥Receive your breath effortlessly as you prepare for sleep tonight. Allow your breath to expand throughout your body to release any tension and pain. Ride the ebb and flow of your breathing until you feel like something else is breathing you. Elevate your awareness into your dream state with every inhale and exhale as you immerse yourself in every dream.

♥Allow your imagination to float into the ethers where you will expand your awareness until you are one with the very essence of your being. It may feel tingly or euphoric, like you're undulating on silk waves of a soft breeze. Just be with this essence that is you, who you are when you're reduced to the very being, the Soul of yourself. There is great value in dropping the ego, personality, thoughts and feelings as you tune into who you are as a divine being. From this place of pure bliss and peace you will sleep deeply and heal completely as you enter the ocean of your dreams. Remember the keys that each dream has for you to unlock the treasures of your life.

♥Breathe deeply and fully to relax your body as you let go of this physical realm tonight. Sink into the recesses of your mind to sleep and restore your body and mind. Reach out by reaching inward to your authentic consciousness the very essence that you are and meet your Soul. Make the connection through your dream travels and expanded consciousness to relax even more. Open your heart and shower yourself with loving then extend that energy of loving beyond your body, your home, your country... and shower all that exists... with your loving.

♥BREATHE DEEPLY and let the Earth realm fall away with each exhale. Tune into your own vibration tonight, your own essence and BREATHE from that awareness. Let things shake loose to open yourself up to receiving more LIGHT more in the way of divine grace. Be open and receive all that can support you, protect you and guide you into your next journey inwardly through your dreams. Become formless and intertwined with the Light... dream from the essence of your being and delight in the wisdom.

♥Sustain yourself tonight with your deep breathing, as you relax enough to fall asleep. Invite your body to heal itself as it restores every cell during the night with each breath. Unfold your consciousness to expand into the etheric realms through the threads of your dreams. Weave in and out, over and around all the symbols, fragments of thoughts, pieces of memory as your dreams integrate all of this into a form of communication. Surrender to a higher power, your inner master, the wisdom of your Soul and keep unfolding into the essence of who you are.

♥Center yourself in your heart and breathe deeply from that loving center. Allow the light to move through you with each breath and open yourself to the adventure awaiting you with each dream. Explore the wonders of Soul Travel as you traverse the inner realms of light and sound and know that this too is sacred. Honor your essence and keep your loving heart open with each breath you take and every dream you have.

♥Embrace the night with fertile dreams as your consciousness branches out reaching further than before. Liberate your Soul to travel throughout the sacred realms as you weave your dream threads together into the tapestry of your life. The deeper you ground yourself and anchor to this world the more freedom you will have to expand into the esoteric realms ascending into greater levels of divine light permeating further within each dream.

♥Take in a deep breath and... Break free tonight. Leave this world behind as you ascend into your dream journey. See with new vision and explore the mystical realms until you remember more and more of whom you truly are, the very essence of your being. Escape what no longer serves you, what you have evolved from and embrace the truth as it is revealed to you in every image, in every way. Breathe deeply and let go and ride your dreams into your Soul.

♥Inhale the sacredness of this night as you exhale the past completely. Become present in the now and drift into your relaxed sleep to drift further into your dream portal and begin your dream sojourn. Float among the stars and shapes of colors that surround you while your dreams stream into worlds without end. From this abstract perspective you will gain new insight and awareness to truths that have gone unnoticed... open your heart, open your Spiritual eyes and ears and travel a sacred path to knowing with each breath you take.

♥REnew by being NEW... as you release this day and inhale the night... breathe deeply of the darkness of this night and prepare yourself for your dreamland by unlearning all that you think you know ...simply LET GO. Empty your mind, clear your emotions relax your body and begin your dream journey. While sleeping your dreams may reveal wisdom and clues to your living the life of your dreams. Pay attention to everything that comes into your consciousness while you're awake and when you're sleeping. Dreams leave clues simply surrender to your essence and breathe.

♥Take in a long deep breath and release it with a humming sound so the vibration relaxes you even more. Zoom into your dreams, as you tumble through the colorful images of your creative mind within the sacred light of your essence. Surrender the need to know to simply expand into greatness which you already are. Allow your dreams reveal the sacred mysteries that are longing to be remembered by your Soul.

♥With each deep breath take in the divine light and release the tensions and worries from today... with each breath draw yourself closer to your Soul. Sweet dreams on your Souls journey through the night. You can actually awaken your awareness as you sleep through reconnecting with your divine essence. Leave your body to rest and restore as you awaken more within each dream. You will remember more each morning and as you put the pieces together the veil will lift and you will awaken more and more. WAKE UP as you fall asleep tonight.

"The breath of God brings life and the loving that you are. It brings the presence of God through all ages, through all time. This breath initiates the healing, the reawakening, and the realization of who you are in the Divine. It is the emanation that awakens all."
~John Morton, D.S.S, "The Blessings Already Are"

Happiness & Joy

For the most part we are born happy and tend to make everyone happy around us! Somewhere along the path of life we burdened our natural state of happiness with worry and concern; while spending too much time in the past or the future in lieu of being here and now. Little children and puppies too are happy; they frolic, laugh, and enthusiastically tackle something new with curiosity and a smile. Let's remember ourselves to our younger years when happy was a way of being.

Joy is the natural state of Spirit... of your Soul. Your Soul is always joyful and when you create a connection with your Soul you experience greater joy. When we are joyful it seems to bubble up from deep inside of us and we are grateful and content with our life in that moment. This category of blessings will nudge your memory to tap into the happy times and bring up the joy inside of you waiting patiently to be expressed. Invite these dream blessings to transport you into another state of mind and start thinking happy thoughts and you just may fall asleep and awaken with a smile on your face.

"When you move to the power source of your beingness in the inner kingdom, you find happiness and joy. It is a dynamic joy, an active expression of happiness. And within that happiness is peace. It may not be jovial or raucous happiness, but it is one where the warmth of your own consciousness is united with the knowingness of your Soul. And when those two aspects are one, happiness is the natural result." ~**John-Roger**

♥Let your Soul travel joyfully through your dreams and beyond tonight. Open your heart to caress the gentle loving of angels as you sleep the night away with a smile on your face. Allow the soft waves of Spirit to anoint you with blessings without end and fill your heart with happiness. Open, explore, discover and know that everything is for you... everything; for you are a SOUL.

♥Choose wisely your thoughts and words as you enter the dream zone. You create your own reality... what do you DESERVE to ENJOY? How do you prefer to live this life? Ponder those answers deep within yourself; integrate all the aspects of your consciousness (subconscious, unconscious, inner child and more) to fully participate in your life on all levels. ABRA CADABRA! And so it is! Bathe yourself in God's grace and allow joyful happiness to transform you.

♥As your body falls deep in restful sleep tonight, smile as you let your energy of light soar to new heights and depths of your Spirit. Take in a deep breath and Be light, colorful and expansive to reach far and wide as you delve inside to the joyful spirit that you are with each dream tonight. Let's all bring forward greater blessings a true happiness to all living beings.

♥Travel through your dreams tonight into places that will leave you in awe, with a gentle comfort of peaceful joy. Leave your mind behind to rest and your physical body to recover while you travel in your body of light. Anoint yourself with the grace of Spirit and partake in the blessings which are waiting for you to receive. Be light, good night, awaken in the morning with awareness and delight.

♥With gentle waves of Spirit bless yourself tonight as you sleep. Rest and dream the night away. Set an intention to re-member yourself to your body of LIGHT as you travel through the inner realms. Release all that may be blocking you from becoming more aware of your joyful, radiant beingness. And know that the blessings already are here.

♥To BE IN THE PRESENT is to give yourself a GIFT. To be in the NOW is to be in the KNOW. Give yourself a gift, BE PRESENT and in the KNOW. STOP... Breathe... Rest and give into the blessings of the night to dream yourself into happiness. Gently let go... go to sleep... wake up in your dreams to the joyful delight that is always present within you and rejoice in the joy that comes present.

♥Make the SHIFT happen tonight as you begin your dreams ...from a place that you thought was "it," to the possibility of what can be far beyond your wildest dreams. Be like water... ever flowing, evaporating and transforming. Be the fog, be the midst, be present to what is possible. DREAM THE NIGHT AWAY and shift your consciousness into other realms of reality way beyond what you think is real. Feel, heal and reveal... the best is yet to come. Smile and know that it will be fun!

♥Dream time is the perfect time to release your Soul to travel the night. Leave your body to rest and heal as you explore and discover more within your body of light and your keen consciousness awareness. Breathe deeply and relax into the essence of yourself and re-member everything you already know for when you connect on this elemental level there is joy present. Receive the gifts that await your claim and indulge yourself in every single dream.

♥Tune into your light tonight as you stream into your dreams. Expand your consciousness beyond the form into the formless, to explore the worlds without end. Create the space necessary to gain greater perspective on it all to allow this expansive space to bring forward content and happiness to you and fine tune your awareness. Open yourself to the miracles at hand ...rest completely and dream sweetly.

♥It's never too early or too late for a blessing. Let your worries and concerns fade away into the yesterdays where they were born. Grace your Soul with a breath of renewal and let your heart sing joyfully with delight. Open your consciousness to travel through the dream worlds tonight and free your thoughts completely. Ride the energy of Spirit into the possibilities and opportunities that are coming your way. Lead the way with your loving and nourish your Soul with staying present.

♥Close your eyes and OPEN YOUR AWARENESS tonight as you fall asleep. There are lights of brilliance and vivid color beyond your imagination. So enjoy the show! Dreams are the vehicle to traverse these realms. Jump in and go. The more you awaken to your higher consciousness, the greater the integration and synergy is available to you. Let everything that is NOT you simply fall away and reveal the REAL authentic true you, which is a state of pure joy.

♥Dance with joy in your dreams tonight, dance to the sound current; the sound you cannot hear with your ears. Let your light shine bright to guide your way through this night. Flow with the vibration of Spirit into your Soul Journey dancing across the bridges of time and the waters of knowledge into the sacred places you will come to know. Dance to your own precious joy-filled rhythm into the heart of God.

♥Remember, tonight as you prepare for sleep, what captured your heart and touched your spirit as a child. Return to the pure essence of who you are and delight in the cherished memories to open your loving happy heart now. Bring that pure joy to your being, your body, your mind and your feelings. Anoint yourself with your own magnificent loving. Breathe, relax and return to yourself as you travel into your dreams... let go and "let's go" the night holds happy treasures for you to discover.

♥Expand your awareness tonight in your Soul flight inside and outside of dreams. As you slowly explore your dreams, observe every detail; for this is when time stands still. Travel deep within your consciousness to discover the treasures that await you and remember what fills your heart with joy and cherished happy memories. Breathe in the calm and cherish it all.

♥Let your heart be light tonight as you enter the dream portal. Dance upon the silk waves of Spirit with your body of light. This process of unfoldment, as you become more aware of the other realms of life and energy, can be exciting, provoking and enlightening. Ask for the light to illuminate your happy consciousness and set yourself free. Rest, restore and renew yourself with every joyful breath.

♥Center yourself in your heart and breathe deeply from that loving center. Breathe in joy and exhale your fear. Allow the light to move through you with each breath and open yourself to the joyful adventure awaiting you with each dream. Explore the wonders of Soul Travel as you traverse the inner realms of light and sound and know that this too is sacred, so just be happy. Honor your essence and keep your loving heart open with each breath you take.

♥Breathe in the light and gently relax as you let this day go. Soar into your dreams with magical wonder. Focus on being joyful and allow yourself to transform in perfect timing. Tonight as you ascend higher and higher, partake in the mystical travels within each dream. The higher you go the more you'll know and the happier you'll become.

♥Embrace the night, embrace the light and dreams of joyful pure delight. Affirm what you deserve to enjoy in your life right here right now, and let everything else fade away. Nocturnal blessings of gentle bliss are yours to receive. Be the beloved that you are and sleep deeply for a healing rest. Open your heart & mind so you can soar with your Spirit and dream the night away to return with a deep contentment.

♥ASCEND this world tonight and catapult yourself in your dream vessel. Let your body rest and sleep while you awaken your consciousness and Soul travel! Journey into the worlds without end to gather the happiness and joy available to you through your dreams. Raise your vibration as you gain more awareness in awakening to all that you already are; for you are on a Soul journey so simply relax, breathe and be happy.

♥During your slumber tonight allow yourself to sink gracefully into your physical body. Exhale slowly so you can lift your body of light into the highest place that you can ascend to. When you reach the point of suspension; sense the quiet, calm, simple, delicate joy. Breathe it in fully and allow that to transform you on every level. Hover and sustain yourself within the peace of your Soul as you travel through your dream voyages and discover what truly is authentic happiness.

♥Close your eyes and open your imagination as you fall asleep tonight. Breathe deeply of the peaceful calm that is present for you to receive. Drift into your dreams with gentle flow and graceful ease as your breath dances on your lips. Dance on the wings of your dreams all night through and discover the joyful mystical mysteries that are waiting for you. Express yourself as a truly happy being.

♥Sacrifice your ego, control and personality tonight and give your Soul permission to choreograph your dreams. Let the joyful energy move you into the deepest sleep so your mystical night journey can begin. Gracefully flow into altered states of dream consciousness; while your essence dances in the ethers of the light with a happy dance. Breathe deeply of this sacred peace and relax into the night and keep dreaming. Awaken with the feeling of happiness.

♥Slip under your covers and sink into your bed; so your body is ready to rest completely. Now zoom, zoom, zoom into your body of light as you cross through the veil into your dream realms. B R E A T H E in joy and relaxation during your mystical journey; while your Soul Travels into the esoteric places where sacred wisdom is waiting for you. Be present, be new, become the real you. When you dream, you awaken to more of the joy inside you.

♥Night journeys into the dream tunnel can be filled with glorious color and light. Each shape is a symbol and if you pay attention, each colorful light has a vibration, and a sound. Follow the sound and light to the deepest place you are aware of. Partake in the happiness of mystical divine perfection. You may find comfort and healing or perhaps feel energized and directed. Follow the path of your dreams each night with wonder and joy. Happiness is a natural state of the authentic you!

♥Ahhh ...BREATHE... ahhh, relax. Become present in the now, right now... and fine tune your awareness to this moment. As you start your depth spiral into your dream sleep world tonight, erase your thoughts and memories to focus on YOU. Open to the possibilities of grace and mystical light-filled miracles as you are transported into the colorful light of images and wisdom with every dream. Enjoy the freedom of this realm. Feel joy as you remember and return with the gems of happiness always within you.

♥Prepare to rest, restore and dream throughout this night as you turn your eyes inward into your true journey. As much joy and wonder you find in our physical world; you will discover even more esoteric and mystical wonders within yourself. Put your mind and feelings to rest, BREATHE DEEPLY, and begin your inward journey as your dreams transport you to another reality so let go of your struggle and be happy, be joyful, be the real you.

♥Learning the language of your body includes your subconscious and unconscious bodies too. Dreams are the language of our subconscious filled with symbols and images that have meaning and significance. Be free and open to explore and observe what your dreams are telling you. Just go with the flow until you know. Lay your head to rest. Let your body connect to your happiness with ease, as you enter the mysterious world of dreamland. Sleep well. Find the joy you seek within your dreams and bring it to your conscious mind. Awaken happy and refreshed!

♥Tell your body to rest and sleep, as you invite your Soul to rejoice and joyfully dance into your dreams. Become like air and float freely into the shapes and colors that beckon you to be free. Focus this creative energy of freedom and grace to every place within your body that may benefit from a healing and balance every cell to impeccable radiant health. Dreams are the gateway to deeper knowledge and wisdom so let go and dream deeply and know that happiness is your true natural state.

♥Like the petals of a flower that close to sleep the night, fold into yourself as you cuddle up to your center. Rejuvenate yourself with the divine light within. Let it radiate outward beyond your body as a healing, balancing, cleansing energy. Now that you are centered and filled with light, step onto a ray of light and transport yourself into your world of dreams. Gently glide along the sacred light inside the inner realms within your consciousness and experience the joy and wonder. Ask your dreams to transport you to experience more happiness in your life now.

♥Breathe in relaxation as you let yourself drift into your dreams tonight. Flash back to a time where you explored with wonder and joy and gathered all those memories in your heart. Invite your inner child to join you in your dream journeys and trek through the jungle of adventure as each dream melts into another. Each dream is a thread which weaves your levels of consciousness together with fascinating mystical magical wonderment. Weave these joyful dreams and allow yourself to enjoy a happier life.

♥Celebrate the NEW in yourself tonight as you clear your mind and open up to a plethora of possibilities. Let your dreams lead you into what can come to be joyful bliss. Our dreams process a myriad of thoughts, unresolved feelings, concerns and new opportunities. Our dreams are able to "work out" many things that may otherwise weigh us down in our day to day life. FREE YOURSELF THROUGH YOUR DREAMS TONIGHT ...begin a NEW YOU in the morning and just BE happy. Now allow your dreams to embrace you with rapture, delight and joyful bliss as you envelop yourself into your dream-world.

"Too much of a good thing can be wonderful!" ~ **Mae West**

FAITH & SPIRIT

You are a divine Soul "trapped" for a while in your physical body. When you forget this you may require faith. Faith is believing and trusting in something that you don't yet know for sure, or perhaps even remember at all. Faith bridges the gap from this world to the sacred divine realms of Spirit. Regardless of religion or having no religion, you are much more than your physical body. That within your consciousness is your Soul. Your inner spirit is what endures everything and your Soul is absolute perfection.

Like an iceberg, your Soul is so tremendously huge that it cannot fit in this tiny package called a human body. The iceberg floats on the water showing only about 10% of its complete size above the water line. When you go deeper into the abyss you can clearly recognize that this iceberg is much larger under the water though it goes unseen by the human eye. Our Soul or Spirit is like that... we fit a small part within our body and the rest is hidden in the deep abyss of consciousness that cannot be seen with the human eye. As you read this collection of nighty-night blessings for your Spirit and Faith your Soul just may appear to you as a lucid dream or a glance in the mirror. This is an awakening process most everyone yearns for.

"The dream is the small hidden door in the deepest and most intimate sanctum of the soul, which opens to that primeval cosmic night that was soul long before there was conscious ego and will be soul far beyond what a conscious ego could ever reach."
~**CARL JUNG "The Meaning of Psychology for Modern Man"**

♥Fill, surround and protect yourself in the sacred light that awaits your request. Breathe in all the goodness, abundance, health and balance you can receive... and exhale all that is not that. Come into your peace pod within yourself and sleep, dream, heal. Receive the blessings that your dreams will offer you to resolve, relieve and refocus all that matters to you. Wrap yourself in the darkness and the unknown until you feel the warm embrace of faith and trust that you are being protected and prepared. It's often darkest before the dawn, have faith and sleep deeply to dream magnificently.

♥It's time to sleep and rest your conscious mind; so the rest of your mind can dream. Breathe deeply into the twilight ethers and merge into your dreams. Listen for the whispers of sound that will carry you into the light. There is always light, just keep going deeper to discover it. Inhale the ethers of the twilight realm. As the misty fog envelops you, journey into your dreams and beyond the mystery schools. Follow the whispering sounds into the light and illuminate your Soul. Your Soul knows and remembers, so let your mind rest and be at ease. This is the time for your inner self to express through your dream voyages.

♥Nighty-night calls you into dream land for a restful healing sleep so your dreams can work for you! Give your thoughts and feelings a break, let them rest and sleep for now. Invite your subconscious process all the unresolved issues of the day as you watch them spin out of your consciousness. Breathe deeply as the clutter is released. Let your Soul soar into and beyond the etheric realms as you receive the wisdom and perfection each dream offers you. The more you practice this, the less faith you'll require as your experience of knowing will replace your faith.

♥Gently surround yourself in a bubble of bright of glowing radiant light. Softly breathe deeply and release the day completely to become totally present in the now. Enter your sleep with a gentle surrender, as you travel into the deepest part of your consciousness. From the seat of your Soul slip into your dream voyages tonight, and traverse the inner and outer realms of light and sound with mystical wonders. Let your body of light connect the dots with each symbol of your dream state and affirm the faith you have with the process you're in.

♥Softly close your eye lids to rest and sleep. Let your body become very heavy to sink into your bed. Have your eyes roll way back into your skull, and gain keen inner sight from the deepest recesses of your awareness. Feel the energy inside your palms and bless your body, your life and all of your situations, concerns and circumstances; so a healing and restoration can occur. When storms appear delight in the sound and light for it anoints new life; in the stressors of your life which gives birth to new possibilities is the blessing. Follow your dreams into your creative center and watch your life unfold in new and miraculous ways. Always follow your dreams.

♥Sleep deeply so you can ascend fully into the dreamy state of Soul Travel. The deeper you sleep the further you can traverse the dream realms and learn, grow and heal. Bask in the light of your Spirit and indulge in every dream scheme to open your consciousness more and more. Breathe, vibrate and attune yourself to the sacred breath which breathes you while you sleep deeply and heal fully.

♥Talk to your fear, doubt and panic like you would speak lovingly to a little child. Calm that part of you who cannot see the light nor feel the faith. Breathe deeply and sustain your breath to fill every part of your body. Release it fully as you release all your worldly concerns. Breathe gently into the rhythm of your heartbeat and float into a deep healing sleep. Journey into your dreams with keen awareness of what becomes present for you to discover and explore. Invite the silk waves of your dream threads to deliver wisdom, wonder and miracles into your life. Pay attention to your nightly dreams, for you are the weaver of the tapestry as you recreate the life you deserve. There are many gems available to you.

♥Bask in the light and Bless yourself tonight with the sacred divine light ...invite the angels to tuck you in as you drift off to a peaceful deep sleep. Surround yourself with healing light, transformational dreams and jettison yourself into a new frequency of vibration in the process of renewal. To experience a new way of being requires faith in the process for it is unknown to you for now... just keep breathing, dreaming and allow yourself to unfold in perfect timing and divine perfection.

♥Surrender to your Soul and ride the energy of Spirit as you delve into your sleep into the deepest place that you can rest in your consciousness... breathe deeply from that place. Release yourself into your dreams and jettison yourself into the light of your Soul and see yourself looking back at you. Trust in the faith that you already have and follow your dreams as they unravel the mysteries within your being.

♥Breathe deeply and hold the breath in until it fills every place in your body. Expand with relaxation and release your breath to relax even more. Focus on your breath and heart beat as you begin to fall asleep in the calm pool of peaceful quiet. Gently your dreams will drift into focus and you will be on your journey. Within each dream, while your body sleeps, awaken more and more. Come into the light with faith and trust as the New Earth is calling those who can hear the plea... wake up and live your dreams!

♥Time to enter your dream vortex and explore new realities within the mystical world's without end. Dive in so far into the dark void that you emerge into the graceful light. Allow your Soul to take flight and remember what you've forgotten. Embrace the rapture of your deep healing sleep and dance into your dreams with delight. Joyfully sparkle as you leap and twirl from dream to dream and let the sound current of vibrations piece them all together. Breathe deeply, relax fully and open to receive the nightly blessings.

♥Grow your mind and explore your imagination by delving into your dreams with faith, anticipation and gratitude. Your dreams speak the language of your subconscious mind... we all deserve to be heard and acknowledged... so listen, watch and enjoy the inner show! Indulge yourself in your deep sleep ...breathe in the light and send it through your body to heal, sleep and rest the night through. Journey into new spaces and places as you ride each dream on the path of discovery with courage and faith.

♥Faith calls upon you as night time asks you to let the day go and fall into your slumber. Breathe deeply and relax even more to surrender into your dreams. Ask to receive the answers you seek so your dreams will know how to guide you. Be embraced by the light while your Soul Travels the realms of mystical wonder as the sweetest most revealing dreams occur when we completely detach from our bodies and thoughts ...breathe deeply and let go, your consciousness is waiting to be reborn again. Enter your light with faith and trust as you sweetly dream.

♥The night whispers "time to sleep" so your dreams can usher you into the mystery schools of wisdom. Breathe deeply and let go of this world so your Soul can travel on the divine thread of light into the worlds without end and dreams can be born from the esoteric realms so your awareness is heightened. Become the colors, shapes and sounds of your dreams as they begin to lure you into their magic. Enter the tunnel of altered states while your body sleeps, your feelings heal and your mind restores itself. Jettison yourself into the worlds without end within your consciousness and learn from the mystery schools of wisdom and knowledge.

♥Time to test your faith and reach beyond your physical form... enter your sleep by releasing this level. Follow the deeper sound calling you into your dreams and surrender your process into Soul travel tonight. With each glimmer of light and symbol in your dreams you thin the veil between here and there. Journey inward to jettison yourself higher into the subtle dimensions of Spiritual realms where your Soul awaits illumination. Let there be light!

♥Tuck yourself into your dream envelope tonight and explore the inner realms of light, color and sound while your body sleeps deeply and restores itself to health. Balance all of your bodies while you dream the night away, your physical body and your subtle bodies too. Have faith that everything you want is within your reach... be willing to reach into places and realms you have yet to discover. Allow your dreams to pull you into the mystical light of lucid wisdom and awaken more with each Ah-Ha moment. Delve deeply into your dream schemes, everything is FOR YOU, so partake and enjoy! Trust that the faith you need is already within you.

♥Take in a moment of trusting in the faith that you have and inhale a deep breath to begin your sleep, let your emotions swirl out of sight and your thoughts fall away like specks of flecks ...breathe in again deeply and slowly as you release into relaxation. As you leave your body to heal while it sleeps, open your imagination to soar into your dreams into the light within. Each dream weaves a thread of wisdom and integrates your inner worlds with this outer world. Balance your body, mind and spirit as each dream transforms you more and more.

♥Render yourself into a deeply relaxing sleep as you surrender everything else and demonstrate faith in your process. Follow your dream fragments as you piece together the puzzle of discovery. As you allow your Soul to travel, the rays of light will protect your journey while you sleep and dream throughout the night. Begin your inner journey within each dream tonight as your body sleeps, heals and balances itself with faith in yourself. Seek the treasures inside of you and you will bestow a wealth of riches to nourish your Soul.

♥Time to enter the caverns of your dreams within dreams and have faith you will be shown the way. Let your mind go and surrender to the lure of imagination to the sacred journeys within as your Soul travels upon the divine threads of light and sound. Sleep deeply now engulfed in the light and dream. Let the pulse of the night rock you into a deeper sleep as you lift into the dream ethers. Listen for the sound that streams like a current of echoes gently awakening; see the light emerge in your consciousness with each dream journey. As your Soul travels through the realms of light your body will resonate with healing vibrations. That you can trust with the utmost faith.

♥Escape this day by embracing the night and rapture of your dreams in your deepest sleep. Peace is what you are as a loving Soul of light, a brilliant glowing light of spirit. Breathe into your essence tonight, delve into the dark of night and release yourself to your dreams. Surf the waves of sound and vibration into each dream fragment and sequence. Give up to receive and dive deeper into your tunnel of dreams which balance you, restore you and heal you on many levels. Breathe into the relaxation and peace of your slumber and glide into your dreams with ease and grace. Watch with wonder of your dream magic and welcome every symbol and image into your life. Anoint yourself in the peaceful sacred light and be healed on all levels.

♥Let go of this day to surrender into the night demonstrate the faith required to earn your own trust ...sink your body into your bed and let it rest to heal. Ascend this level to float into your dreams and traverse the inner realms of wonder and awe. Gather the dream gems as you drift along to absorb the wisdom of your Soul travel tonight. Be light, be the light because you are light. Go to your inner sanctuary tonight and bathe your body in the healing light and release your Soul to travel. Invite your dreams to sweep you away into the deepest levels of wisdom within the mystery schools as each dream lures you to discover more. Anoint yourself with sacred sound and return in the morning renewed, refreshed and aware.

♥Who breathes you when you sleep? What awakens in your dream when you're unconscious? That is the faith you'll need to take you to the next step, your next level. Take a moment to relate and connect to all that you see and know to remember that you are not alone. Invite your dreams to lift you into the essence of who you are through the esoteric realms of divine wisdom and illuminate yourself with the radiant light. Take time to be generous with yourself and focus on your inner peace. Bless yourself with gratitude and grace yourself with your divine light of loving radiance. Release the day, your life and drift into your dreams as you sleep and restore. Gems of wisdom await your discovery inside of every dream you have.

♥Travel the waves of light and sound into the images of your inner mind and emerge with profound wisdom and faith. Take in a deep breath and sustain it in your lungs to relax you at deeper levels. Now, gently exhale with a releasing sound. Let your body sink deeply into your bed and gently put your mind and emotions to rest as you float into your sleep. Begin your dream journey with total trust as your Soul travels the night weaving through each dream in divine perfection weaving threads of light, faith and wisdom just for you.

♥Your sleep beckons you to enter your dream gate and traverse the inner realms as you ascend into the light. Breathe deeply yet gently of this subtle aromatic air to fill yourself with healing grace. Surround yourself in spirals of light as you faithfully prepare for dreamland in your sleep tonight. In your dream vessel express your gratitude for the life you have and share what you can so you can openly receive. Ask for what you deserve to enjoy; a healing, more abundance and deeper connection with others. Whatever it is, ask and let your dreams deliver. Ascend this worldly level tonight and rise into your beacon of light as you let go and let God.

♥Beloved, leave your fears, tears and pain behind as you launch your Soul into your dreams tonight. Demonstrate the faith you have and are to allow this gift to be yours. You are the vessel in which your dreams will be filled. Be open, dance freely in your spirit to receive the blessings. The more you release and let go the more you will invite a complete healing process. Follow your heart and dreams into the next possibility. Dance on the waters of delight for all is possible through your surrender and trust. You are never alone... so let go of the struggle and sleep deeply while your dreams come alive tonight.

♥Sparkle in your dreams like a flickering candle of light and champion yourself in every way. Have faith that you are a winner and you deserve to win and it's your dreams so WIN in each one of them. Open yourself to receive fully of the brilliance and passion of your own inner light! Surrender to your sleep, bathe your body in sacred holy healing light and take off into your dreams. Become a neutral observer as you traverse the inner worlds without end into and through each dream you have. Observe and receive all the blessings being bestowed to you now.

♥Have faith and surrender to the night let it engulf you and swallow you whole. Float gently into your sleep and weave into your dreams to create the tapestry of your life on the inner realms. Each thread of your dream carries a vibration of healing, completion and majesty of what you may become in your evolution. Envelop yourself in the rapture of nature and release it all to embrace this blessing. Neutrality is the state you will set yourself free! Be present with the gift of "NOW" and launch your Spirit to explore the dimensions of the sacred world of dreams. Set sail to explore the inner realms of worlds without end and relish in the wonder and awe of what is possible for you to become.

♥Invite the light to surround you, illuminate and fill you with balance, health and abundance. Breathe deeply of this sacred light and anoint your beingness with each breath. Softly close your eyelids and melt into your bed as you float away to sleep. Welcome your dreams with gratitude for the healing transformation they offer. Open the floodgates of your dream world, and drop it all to soar into your Soul body and traverse the realms of worlds without end. Every image, color, light and sound carries a seed of wisdom for you to cultivate and nurture. Love yourself enough to let yourself grow and let your spirit unfold.

♥Connect with your inner universe tonight... see the light with your inner eye, track the sound from deep within and follow. Forget this world, let it fade away and fall into your deep slumber to heal and restore your body. Float into your dreams with awe and trust every image and symbol is set up for you to win. Trust in the Spirit and Soul within the core of who you are and have faith it will lead you where you need to be.

♥Breathe deeply and release it all... let it all go, now. Become so present with yourself now that you hear sound in the silence and see light in the darkness. Sleep is ready to engulf you in its gentle arms so your body can heal, your mind can be free and your emotions can flow like water. Shed a tear to anoint yourself as you enter your dreams with wonder and awe... Embrace it all, accept it all and love it all as you renew yourself each day. This night invites you to surrender the day and renew yourself as you delve into your dreams to set your Soul free to traverse the realms of worlds without end. Reconnect yourself to your source, your light, your Spirit... and have faith that your journey of discovering the endless wisdom available to you is indeed possible.

♥Soften your body into a puddle of relaxation and melt into your sleep with gentle joy for your Soul yearns to travel with freedom. Release your energy into your dreams and follow where they lead you into greater depths of light filled wisdom and integration gliding on the energy within each dream. Let your mind flow like a stream as your head rests on your pillow tonight and you slip into a deeply relaxing sleep. Allow your dreams to unravel all your feelings and thoughts into the images of "dream talk" and observe as the magic unfolds. Dreams are very healing so relax, release, and recover while you sleep the night away.

"What we experience in dreams – assuming that we experience it often- belongs to the end just as much to the over-all economy of our soul as anything experienced 'actually': we are richer or poorer on account of it." ~**Friedrich Nietzsche, Beyond Good and Evil**

Holidays & Celebrations

Oh how we look forward to events that invite celebrations in our lives. Times to reconnect with friends and gather with family, times to give, receive, bless and honor our lives and traditions. Holidays are splendid! Special events that occur with the seasons and nature phases are also milestones to treasure with acknowledgment and celebration. Reaching a milestone worth celebrating for optimum health, landing that job, reaching your goal are all achievements worthy of celebrating.

It's joyful to remember yourself as a child during your favorite holidays and cherish those experiences as you celebrate those same holidays today. Birth and Birthday celebrations, Weddings and Anniversary's plus all the family and school reunion's also make celebrating worth celebrating! Even our monthly moon phases can offer causes to celebrate too. Be present in the moment, look up your favorite holiday and celebrate with each passing month what you treasure most about your amazing life. Your precious life is worth celebrating every day!

"Dream on it. Let your mind take you to places you would like to go, and then think about it and plan it and celebrate the possibilities. And don't listen to anyone who doesn't know how to dream."
~Liza Minnelli

Moon Phases:

♥OH MAGNIFICENT MOON… please scoop me up into your brilliant light and take me away to dreamland far, far away. Lure me into the vast void of dark empty space so that I can breathe fully and expand with your energy to transform the abyss into magnificent possibilities of mystical wonder. I dream with my eyes closed and I dream with my eyes wide open for my dreams take me where I discover who I truly am.

♥The dreamy night of the FULL moon's light lures us to the mysteries within. As you close your eye lids and enter the dark void let the light of this moon send rays of light to guide your pathway into your dreams. This moon expands us, opens our awareness and swells our planet too. Be open to receive the gifts your dreams offer and to sleep well and awake wiser in the morning.

♥Give into the Full Moon tonight, let it draw you closer, let go and drift into greater surrender. Healing energy is present for you so simply just breathe and partake in the blessings. Float away in your dreams and discover what is true and unique to you. Honor yourself in every way and integrate all that you know without knowing how or why. It is time for all of us to shine our light on all the shadows and dance in the light of Spirit together in harmony and joy.

♥FULL Blood MOON: Open yourself to the pull of this Full Moon …a Blood Moon at that. Can you palpate the energy shift and the quickening urging you to take greater action? Hop on the transformation transportation and become a part of something bigger than yourself. Step up on the brilliant radiant moon ray and transport yourself beyond your dreams into fulfillment into manifesting your dreams for your life. Time to MAKE YOUR DREAMS COME TRUE!

♥Bask in the FULL MOON tonight and wrap yourself in the protection of the light. Strengthen your core with affirming who you authentically are as a Spiritual being of light, as a human being, as all the other roles you play in your life. Return to your source and renew your body and Soul with every breath. Follow your dreams and release everything that may be blocking your progress... delve into your dreams to see with your inner eye and your imagination. Anoint yourself from this sacred place of pure peace and expansive calm. All is well. Trust your process.

♥Breathe in the darkness of this night and allow yourself to be lured by this SUPER FULL MOON who is pulling you towards her like the outstretched arms of a loving mother. Embrace your own light and dance on the ribbons of sound which vibrate healing tones for your Soul as you weave your way through the worlds without end from dream to dream.

♥Let the light of this rare Blue Moon pull you into the fullness of possibilities as you jump into your dreams. Trust your intuition as the wisdom comes into focus and your body lifts past all pain and limitations ...set yourself free and keep dreaming the whole night through. Surrender to the light of this magnificent BLUE MOON and become the very ether of which you breathe into each dream tonight.

♥Allow this New Moon to renew YOU! Breathe gently and let the night envelop you in comfort and hug you all night. As your eyes rest and sink into the void you will begin your fantastic voyages through the dream tunnel. Jettison yourself as your Soul travels weaving through your dreams into esoteric mysteries revealed. Sleep peacefully and dream magically as the darkness of the new moon gives birth to new experiences, new ideas and a new you too.

♥As this NEW moon pulls and releases the magnetic energies your consciousness waxes and wanes with awareness. Tonight, in this new moon phase, open to receive and declare what you desire and deserve to enjoy and experience in this life. This "kenosis" of emptiness with the new moon creates a void and an empty canvas which YOU are the painter, so create what you want. Travel through your dreams to uncover the mysteries that haunt you. All is revealed as you open your eyes. Happy Soul Travel tonight within each dream.

♥The blessing of a new beginning is here with this NEW MOON. Like the waves of the ocean erases the writing and castles in the sand, this New Moon will erase your past offering you a clean slate to start over. Forgive yourself for any shame, guilt and judgments or regrets you may have to free yourself and be engulfed in this NEW era of new beginnings. Ride your dreams into the possibilities of a "do-over" month and breathe your dreams into your reality. Open yourself to receive the blessings your dreams are bringing to you and renew your life right here and right now.

♥NEW MOON = new beginnings! IF you're anxious, it's time to JOURNAL and write your thoughts on paper. BREATHE, BREATHE, BREATHE and return to the center of your being often as you release what no longer serves you. Let go of the past. Surrender your conditioning to usher in and embrace the NEW YOU for your dreams are preparing you for new adventures with this New Moon light. Float into the new energy this new moon is offering you and allow your dreams to come true.

♥ Lift your Soul up into the light of this Crescent Moon as you lay down to sleep through the night. Let your dreams be the magic carpet that transports your awareness into and through worlds without end. Remember the fragments and pieces of your dreams that will seed the possibilities for your tomorrows. Heal yourself with the vibrational of sound and the radiant light as you journey through this very night. Break free tonight as the stars are aligned to gift you with your desires.

♥As the Moon waxes and wanes each month; dissolve yourself, your ego, personality, thoughts and feelings tonight and breathe in calming peaceful glow of illumination. Peacefully drift into your dreams and trust your process. Honor yourself by allowing your dreams to lead the way and build your foundation of trust each night. Tune into a transformational night of dreams as the moon beams light up your path.

New Year and Holidays of Light, Miracles and Gratitude

♥Embrace this NEW YEAR and all the BLESSINGS THROUGHOUT THE NIGHT, while you sleep, rest and renew. Indulge yourself during your revealing dreams about your Spiritual light and gifts. Take a minute to share your blessings and gratitude at least with yourself. Breathe in the possibilities of dreams come true for you in this New Year! You are renewing yourself, a new beginning and celebrating the new you.

♥Tonight celebrate the time of renewal, spring and the sacred holiday of Holy miracles. Escape your body and this physical world by BREATHING in the sacred divine light and take off! Enter into a space, a place where you know all is perfect, calm and peaceful. This is your source, your center of being and from this stillness expand into your dream state. Enter into the ethers with each breath through the inner words without end; as you travel in your Soul to the mystery schools of ancient knowledge. Explore what is present for you to discover and devour the blessings with rapture and gratitude.

♥Sleep well this Sacred holy night, let the angels touch your heart, receive more blessings in your life, loving light to all. Soothe your body and soul with relaxing breathing and invite your dreams to balance you on all levels. Be touched by the angels of grace during this festival of light and bask in the divine holy light tonight in your dreams. Let your Soul soar higher within each dream tonight.

♥Fill yourself with GRATITUDE and THANKFULNESS for your wonderful life. Look for the blessings in disguise when you perceive things to be less than wonderful it will bring you into balance. LIFE IS GOOD, LIFE IS PRECIOUS we all count! HAPPY THANKSGIVING TO YOU ALL, let your day be filled and overflowing with blessings of gratitude. Gratitude is a gift you can give to yourself in every moment... it fills the heart and soothes the Soul.   Sleep well and dream wonderfully.

♥Gently close your eyes and relax deeply into your sleep tonight. Invite the angels to touch close to you as they are so very near on Christmas Eve. The veil between Heaven and Earth is so very thin at this sacred time. You have but to ask and invite then behold. Bask in the divine light and traverse the dream realms with awe and reverence for this is the time many seeds are planted. Cultivate your Soul awareness and watch your dreams grow right here on Earth. Be anointed with the light of the Christ and receive the authentic blessing.

♥Invite the angels close to you this holiday of LIGHT, ask for a blessing and receive your prayer answered. Your Soul is sacred so honor your divinity with transforming your awareness from this physical level into your own light; happy Soul travel for this is the time when Angels touch to the Earth closer than your next breath. Delight in the festival of LIGHT.

Winter, Spring, Summer, Fall

♥Happy Dream Time tonight with the longest night of the year, Winter Solstice! Take in a deep healing breath and let it all go as you enter the darkness to discover the light within. Indulge in this longest night of darkness and peace. Set your intention for what you desire to create from this point onward, and let your dreams lead the way. Rest well while creating your masterpiece in the dream realms for dreams do come true.

♥Spring is renewal and beginning so ESCAPE your body tonight as you fall asleep... leave your body to gently heal itself, calm the pain, regenerate the cells AS YOU JUMP through your dream gate! B R E A T H E and be aware of the essence of pure light and energy that you are and vibrate into the colorful realms of pure light to learn more about who you truly are. Fill, surround and protect yourself with the Spirit as you bask in the new territories that you are discovering. Resonate with the sound you hear without your physical ears, reconnect to all that you are to re-member, all that you are.

♥May your dreams unravel more mysteries through the night of the long Summer Solstice while you Soul Travel the realms of light. Program your mind with the Universal Mind. Meditate on good thoughts and good things will prevail. Find your center, where you are silent and breathe from that place; as you prepare for a healing sleep with significant dreams. Be open and relaxed to receive the treasures of your summer-time dreams!

♥It's harvest time, time to reap what you have sown; Time to give THANKS. Tonight tell your body to rest, heal, renew and sleep a long restful sleep. Tell your Soul to release and travel the night through. Catch a dream and transport your consciousness into the deeper realms of YOU. Relax and enjoy the dream-time journey through the vast depths of subtle energies. They may reveal a more real world to you than you realize now. LET GO, LET GOD, LET IT BE... beloved, sweet dreams.

Birthdays, Weddings, Anniversaries, Reunions, New Starts

♥BIRTH is a time to welcome a new Soul to this Earth plane… a warm welcoming of new life to open your heart fully. Take in a breath tonight, like your very first breath you took when you were born as you look into the precious eyes of this little baby. Honor your life with gratitude. Acknowledge your precious Soul and whisper to yourself what you're thankful for as you drift off to sleep. Watch your dreams display a collage of reflections and glimpses into the future; as you reconnect with the pure essence of a new born baby. Relax fully and simply become present in the moment for that is where dreams become real.

♥Happy Birthday, TO ME! Before you drift off to sleep on your birthday, take a look in the mirror and sing "Happy Birthday" to yourself! Really acknowledge the authentic real you inside of you with reverence and gratitude. Come into a presence of reverence for your life, for all that is you. Fill yourself up with loving gentle celebration on your birth-day. As you close your eyes, let your body melt into your bed as your dreams take flight. Dreams carve the pathway to the esoteric realms where we are honored and embraced ESPECIALLY on our BIRTHDAY. So lay back and enjoy your journey as you celebrate your special day, your own birthday.

♥WEDDING: Sometimes it's hard to fall asleep when you're filled with so much anticipation and excitement! It may have been years in the planning and soon the WEDDING will be here! NOW is the time to focus on each breath you take, listen to your heartbeat and become empty in your mind and emotions. Take long deep breaths to soothe your body and let it release into a puddle of relaxation. In lieu of thinking about the "big day" simply redirect your attention to the light within you, towards your own Soul as you continue to breathe deeply. Let your Soul ascend as you drift off to sleep into the realms of light and divine Spirit embracing the loving of yourself and your beloved you are to marry…as you begin your dream sojourn. Let it all go to be so very present, that is the true gift. Peace be still.

♥Happy ANNIVERSARY! Another year to celebrate a commitment, a goal, a dream which you succeeded in making come true. Take some time to quietly reflect on what you've accomplished during this past year, how far you've come, what you overcame, how you endured and the lessons you've learned. Anoint yourself with appreciation and bless yourself with gratitude as you prepare for a restful healing sleep. Drift into your dreams with a smile and let each dream lift the veils of mystery and wonder to reveal the lucid truth in the most magnificent ways. Celebrate yourself in every way as you look forward to another year of discovery, joy and personal growth as you fade into your sweet dreams tonight.

♥MARRIAGE is a sacred union of two people becoming one in loving consciousness and commitment. The more you keep yourself as a clear channel for loving energy to flow though the greater contribution you will make to your marriage. Focus on yourself before you fall asleep, take time to breath into every part of your body especially if it hurts. Send your healing breath through all of your thoughts and feelings and wipe them all clean as you wash them away with your healing breath. Come into this moment and be present with your awareness... just observe neutrally. Begin to bless yourself on every level and open your heart to embrace the night as you drift off to a deeply healing sleep. Seed your dreams with your loving and send light to your partner and your marriage as your dreams begin to take you away. Traverse the magical mystical dream threads into the world without end; and grace your being with the sacred wisdom that comes into focus for you and your beloved.

♥REUNIONS reunite us with our friends and family to offer time to care, share and joyfully remember. A wonderful time to reflect on who "am I" and how life has evolved. Zoom into your memories and breathe in loving to each one, caress yourself with adoration for your connection with this reunion. Your Soul longs for a reunion with Spirit so slip into a deep sleep, let your dreams wander and reunite with the presence of Divine light. Anoint yourself with the treasures of your life in this world and the worlds without end within your consciousness. Explore the gratitude and joy in your heart as you reconnect with friends and family in this world and celebrate your reunion with the deepest essence of your being... drift away into your dreams with appreciation and gratitude for your life.

♥NEW BEGINNINGS often start with completions and endings. Graduation, employment, relocation, vocation, divorce and school admissions... all mark a milestone of one phase ending to allow another new phase to begin. This can bring on mixed emotions of saying good-bye to the past and embracing the unknown of the future, something new for you. Like the cycle of life all over our planet a new beginning must follow some sort of ending and completion. Looking back at your past with reverence, appreciation, acknowledgement and gratitude for all the lessons learned will assist you in standing on a solid platform and usher you into your next adventure in life. You may want to place your right hand on your belly and your left hand on your forehead as you lay down for a restful sleep. Calm your inner child with words, thoughts and images of pleasant new experiences to look forward to. Breathe fully and deeply to assure yourself that you are safe, protected and ready for this new experience. Ask your dreams to lead you into new pathways with your new beginning, be open to discover your next step in this process. Embrace being the new you and let your sweet dreams lead you into new discoveries of celebration and joy.

♥CELEBRATE...you! There is no need to wait for a date or occasion to take pause to simply celebrate the joyful abundance and blessings in your life... every day can be a reason to celebrate! As you prepare for the night to sweep you away to dreamland, you may consider writing down what you're grateful and thankful for. Journal the blessings in your life that you recognize and appreciate and invite the positive flow of positive energy to engulf you as you fall asleep. You will then ride the energy of positive light swiftly into your amazing dream sojourn into the most amazing places you can imagine. Take it all into your being for you are being shown exactly what you need to support you in this life...sleep, dream...heal.

"What reason do I need to celebrate life? A birthday, a wedding anniversary or a holiday are all reminders that there is something to celebrate. Yet every day can be a celebration of life. I celebrate life by praising God. Praise can be a quiet time of communion with God or a joyous hymn of thanksgiving to God. I celebrate by recognizing the life of God within others. We are all unique expressions of God's creativity and I treat others with all the honor that I would great masterpieces, for indeed we are. I rejoice in every expression of life I perceive. The song of a bird, the beauty of a mountain, the fragrance of a flower, the softness of a kitten's fur all give me reasons to celebrate life." ~ **Author Unknown**

Judith Ternyik

Health & Balance

When we are out of balance emotionally, mentally or physically there is often a point where our bodies will create dis-ease and illness. This may be a very challenging process for many to endure and prepare to receive a solid night's sleep. With so many questions as to why this illness has you or perhaps you're yearning for balance, we tend over think the condition and actually create even more imbalance.

When you give up and surrender your mentalizing about it and ask your dreams to deliver messages to you about your illness you may begin to experience balance and understanding. When you dream your conscious mind is still, quiet and sleeping. Your subconscious mind revs up to process your request, concern and prayers so your dreams will begin to show you images, symbols and information that your conscious mind might otherwise dismiss. Allow each dream blessing to bathe you in relaxation so you can tune into a deep, restful, healing sleep as your dreams come into focus.

"Sleep is that golden chain that ties health and our bodies together."
~ **Thomas Dekker**

♥Breathe in the night and wrap yourself in the darkness as you drift to sleep. Bathe yourself in the light of the moon to release any pain or areas that may be stuck and allow the healing to begin. Lift your awareness beyond the parameter of what you know to soar high above what you thought was real and dream in full color tonight. Expand your consciousness far beyond worlds without end to discover more mysteries of your life and receive healing and balance within each dream voyage. Be present in each breath, that's the real gift.

♥The Universe is always listening... YOUR PRAYERS ARE ANSWERED. Prayers are not only what you express and focus on before you go to sleep at night. Your prayers are also your daily thoughts and mind chatter throughout each day. Energy Follows Thought. Be mindful of your daily mantras for your "prayers" will be answered.

♥Sleep well tonight, rest completely and restore your body to vibrant health. Allow your mind and emotions to take a break as your consciousness explores the nightly travel through your dreams. Trust your process as you learn more about the realms of consciousness not normally seen daily with our usual senses yet so very apparent during our dream state and allow yourself to heal completely and restore yourself into balance.

♥Take a minute to listen to yourself and pray out loud. Bless everything with HEALTH, WELLNESS, HEALING and TRANSFORMATION for each person, animal and plant on our Mother Earth. Extend your heart strings to embrace all of God's creation with your gentle blessing. May the sweetest dreams awaken your consciousness tonight to the next level; as we approach living heaven on Earth together in harmony. Blessings of gratitude, healing and magical dreams, while you listen to the sound vibrating deep within your Soul.

♥When you lay down to sleep invite the night into your consciousness. Sink deeply into your cozy bed and let your body be anchored in total rest. Find the tranquil place of peace within you and stay there a while. Drift peacefully into your dream journey now. Breathe and let go as you enter the light vortex of healing grace, delving even deeper into each dream.

♥Bless you this night as you lay to rest and drift into your essence; while you surrender to your dreams. Create and allow the space to open you into greater relaxation and healing, as you transform your energy into less dense places. Fill, surround and protect yourself with the LIGHT of SPIRIT, as you enjoy your journey into the night. Make a request, a wish, a prayer and declare it so. Plant a seed of possibility for yourself tonight. Rest completely, and in the morning awake renewed. God blesses you in every way, every day. Sleep well with your dreams.

♥Invite the magic of the night to make everything all right. Ask your dreams to reveal the way, and give you keys to resolve any blocks or concerns. Bask in the light of your Spirit and float into a deep restful slumber as you explore other realms of wisdom and wonder. Embrace your loving as you create your own vortex of protection and energy to attract to you what you deserve to manifest. Sleep well, heal and renew, awaken to a brighter light of divine awareness.

♥Listen tonight to the sound of your own breathing and heartbeat. Listen to your thoughts as they fade away then really LISTEN FOR THE SOUND CURRENT, the music of your Soul, the song of God as you travel in your dreams as the vehicle to worlds within worlds. Let the harmonics heal you and feel the vibration of sound loosen what no longer serves you. Resonate with a higher frequency that is the Light and Sound of God. Cuddle up in the veil of Spirit and sleep well tonight.

♥Anchor yourself in the center of your peaceful heart tonight as you let the day fall away. Breathe in the gentle night and calm yourself. Nurture yourself on all levels and simply love yourself. From this center of clarity and stillness you will begin your dream time, and travel into deeper levels of your consciousness. Simply take notice to what you see and what you hear. For the dream visions in the night whisper our future to us in miraculous ways and offer a myriad of ways to come into balance and heal on all levels.

♥Balance is a continual process. The Earth tips more every year, walking is a process of more off balance than on balance. Tonight challenge yourself to balance your thoughts by emptying them. Balance your emotions by accepting all that you feel. Balance your physical body by letting it become very heavy; sinking deeply into your bed as you lift your light-body upward beyond the confines of your room. Swing to and fro as you float and drift into your dreams. Perhaps balance is finding the depth of your Self, the core of your Soul. From that still place you will find balance. Love reaches out to all. Rejoice as you take it in and receive all the blessings available to you.

♥Blessings of LIGHT and ALIGNMENT tonight as you drift to sleep and enter your dream reality. Become the light that you are; so that you radiate far and wide to bring your awareness and energy into places that were hidden from you. Brighten your life with your divine light. Bless all that you are and everyone you know Ride the sound and light of Spirit as a silk wave of energy, which envelops everything everywhere. You are eternal, divine and …perfect… sweet dreams.

♥As you drift off to sleep invite your body to rest and heal. Breathe deeply and relax tonight through as your Soul begins the journey through the dream realms. Observe what you see and the sounds you may hear, and take it all into your beingness. Float along with the current of energy into and through the worlds of light and beyond, where the sacred healing light awaits your arrival. Enjoy these esoteric trips and awaken your consciousness as the mystical moments reveal what your essence yearns to know.

♥Drift through your dreams into the ethers of Spirit. Let the veils fall away layer by layer until it reveals the core of who you are as a divine being of radiant light. From this authentic perspective, you will gain such insight that you can heal your body in one breath. You can balance your life in the blink of an eye. Rest and restore yourself tonight with a luscious deep sleep; as your Soul awakens and travels the realms of light and sound. Now take in a deep breath and release it with a gentle sigh... Gently release your thoughts and enter your dreams with joy and wonder.

♥Gain a new perspective by moving your awareness deep within yourself, so you can travel far beyond what you think you know. From this new reference point many things may come into focus and perhaps even fall away. Lift into the light tonight, as you travel the dream stream into your Soul Awareness to transform yourself with goodness in all ways. Jettison yourself beyond the worlds without end until you remember what you already know. Bask in the loving light to heal yourself in all ways.

♥Tune into your body and focus on areas that are out of balance. Bring your light and your attention to the places that hurt. Place your hands on areas of your body and infuse that place with divine light, love and warmth. Asked to be healed and heal yourself with your own divinity and vibration of light as you expand your energy you will set yourself free. Lift up beyond this physical realm so you can travel through your dreams into other places which also need healing. Through your giving you shall receive so know thyself and heal thyself.

♥Open your heart completely so your light radiates throughout your body. Breathe in the calm and let this night tuck you in for a gentle peaceful sleep. Open your mind and travel on the rays of light, which stretch out from your core center to and beyond the worlds without end. Allow yourself to heal and restore so you return to balance and vitality. You are the light that guides you through the night. Close your eyes and dream deeply, give yourself permission to heal.

♥Inhale all the blessings you can imagine as you breathe deeply. Exhale all the past and concerns you may have... be present here and now. Fall asleep with a sense of adventure as you jettison yourself into your dream journey, into the inner cosmos. Embrace the light and let it illuminate your way as you deepen your awareness in your conscious awakening. Gather the gifts your Soul travels avail to you this night; and create an amazing life for yourself with them.

♥Tuck yourself in tonight with a lullaby of gratitude for everything in your life that is good and wonderful. Set the tone of your dreams with a positive vibration of harmony and happiness by blessing your body, yourself and your life. Open your Spiritual Heart and ask the radiant divine light to fill, surround and protect you as your eyes close for a restful sleep. Let loving lead the way into your dream journey, and partake in the banquet table of possibilities every dream offers you.

♥Extend grace to yourself tonight as you stretch out and gently relax into your slumber. Elevate your awareness and tune into the magnificence of the greater scope of your world. Keep lifting your consciousness up and drift gently into your dreams with a finer attunement to the sacred mystical sounds, that lure you into esoteric discoveries. Ascend into the harmonic frequency of pure Spirit and let yourself be healed and restored. Happy Soul travel during your sweet dreams tonight.

♥Bathe yourself in sacred light tonight allowing this light to calm and soothe your body for a peaceful slumber. Breathe deeply of this sacred light and infuse your lungs and heart with radiant rays of healing light. Let it permeate every cell of your being. Lift your consciousness into the foggy mist of your dream gate, and drift into the mystical magic of your nightly discourses. Ride your dreams to completion and allow them to integrate and balance you on all levels, so you'll awaken with your wisdom of how to heal yourself.

♥Wrap yourself up in the rapture of dreams tonight and invite that process to heal you on all levels. Ask for clarity and direction with divine intervention as you delve into your dream state. Open your awareness and all of your senses to experience the subtle nuances of this altered state of consciousness. Merge with your dreams to deepen your healing process, trust your adventure and enjoy your journey into the esoteric mystical realms. Make enjoying a continual state of homeostasis and affirm your worthiness to receive.

♥In the stillness of the night move to the center of your peace. Listen to the silence and watch the shifting energy like a kaleidoscope of images overlapping as you surrender to your sleep. There is a soft whisper in the sound of silence which carries great wisdom so listen to the sound current within. Observe your dreams as they emerge and follow the puzzle pieces into place like a mosaic image of artistry. Your life is being revealed with each dream so relax, surrender, breathe and listen. With each discovery and new breath; you will gain health and balance.

♥Fold yourself into a deep sleep as you breathe deeply to unfold into your dreams. Open your energies to release your form, your body, your concerns and let that all drift away and expand into the light where healing, renewal and balance may occur. Float upon the essence of your Soul as you ride your dreams like silk waves of spirit through every nuance of each dream this whole night long.

♥Center yourself with the gratitude of this day by acknowledging all the goodness, blessings and learning you experienced. Let your eyelids relax and breathe deeply as you release this physical world to joyfully jump into your dream world! Shine your light brightly though the levels of consciousness into the mystical realms as you ride the energy of each dream into the fullness of what it offers you. Enjoy the ride, the journey and discovering the more subtle parts of you. Let the healing begin!

♥Embrace the beauty in you and give thanks for the goodness in your life as you bathe yourself in pure light. With a heart full of gratitude relax into your sleepy night, as you release this day and float into your dreams. Heal every part of you that hurts. With each sweet dream, partake in the blessings of light and sound that caress you in every moment. Wrap yourself up in a cocoon of gratitude and sleep the night away and travel into all your dreams with healing light.

♥Invite your dreams to unravel the mysteries of your unresolved issues, so you will be set free. Sleepy dream time avails miracles of healing and balancing on a multitude of levels. BREATHE deeply and let it all go as you enter your restful state. Allow your dreams to solve and resolve dilemmas that haunt you while you're awake. Follow the light and sound of divine intervention, and know that you are sacred and protected always. Watch your dreams work it all out for you... to balance and heal you on all levels.

♥Align yourself with the presence of Spirit as you experience your own divinity for your blessings already are, here and now. Make the connection through your dream travels and expanded consciousness then relax even more. Open your heart and shower yourself with loving then extend that energy of loving beyond your body, your home, your country ...and shower all that exists... with your loving. Loving is the key to care for yourself in the highest way possible, love yourself now.

♥Deep sleep is a recipe for a healthy life. Attain the best night's sleep with an easy ritual of healthy balance and preparation. Like changing the channel on TV, just switch yourself to a relaxed open state of being and invite the healing to begin. Drift off into your dreams and explore the deeper layers of healing for you. Sleep, Dream and Heal.

♥Bathe your body with cleansing breaths and healing light as you prepare for sleep. Place your hands and awareness on any pain, blocks or discomfort you may have and send your loving energy through your hands to soothe and heal. Open to your dream portal and travel into the realms beyond your body ...now... sleep sweetly for your dreams are on the way.

♥BREATHE, SLEEP, HEAL ...and travel to the mystery schools in your dreams tonight. Expand your loving essence to embrace all of your experiences; past, present and future. Radiate into uncharted places and discover more of who you are. Focus on your loving heart and resonate with the vibration of your heartbeat for that is the rhythm of your life. Listen to the sound current as you dream until you hear it while you're awake. There is so much more for you... so much more.

♥INHALE the goodness of divine light and let it fill your body and as you exhale, release everything which inhibits health, happiness and peace. Reconnect with your Spirit and ask you Soul what it needs right now. Reconnect with who you truly are as you restfully relax into your sleep. Disconnect your ego, thoughts or concerns and jettison yourself into and beyond worlds without end as you ride the mystical wave of rolling dreams into your restoration, health and balance.

"You have the power to heal yourself, and you need to know that. We think so often that we are helpless, but we're not. We always have the power of our minds. Claim and consciously use your power." ~**Louise Hay**

Self-Care & Healing

Our demanding world burdens many of us with "shoulds" throughout the day in an effort to take care of others, lots of responsibilities all without considering ourselves first. When we continue to give from an empty cup we deplete our energy and our health suffers. We are no longer able to be resilient and bounce back and the pressures of life engulf us like a choke hold.

Taking time each evening for YOU... by taking some personal nurturing time to tune into yourself, focus on healing and caring for what you require is essential for your well-being. Each night as you invoke a blessing of caring for yourself, honoring your Spirit and dedicating time to connect with your essence your body often responds with a state of relaxation. We sleep best when we attain a relaxed state before we drift off to dream land. As you set an intention to take better care of yourself and pay attention to your own needs so you are better able to cope and succeed in this world.

"Rest and self-care are so important. When you take time to replenish your Spirit, it allows you to serve others from the overflow. You cannot serve from an empty vessel." ~ **Eleanor Brown**

♥Fall into the light of Spirit tonight as you fall asleep... Release your pain, surrender your suffering, let it all go. Transform and heal yourself with each deep breath and renew every cell in your body with divine alignment. Stretch your awareness far beyond your physical body and limitations and know that you are divine. Become endless with the essence of who you are in all that splendor. You are a sacred thread of God, honor that and expand your loving and be healed.

♥Lay your body down gently to rest and sleep tonight, heal completely with a gentle calm. AND energize your Spirit to rise above this level through the dream gate into Soul Travel... you are a body of light, of energy and can travel faster than the speed of light. Expand your awareness and learn all that you can, the night is short yet the opportunities are endless. Extend your energy as far as you can for it will return fruitful and abundant.

♥Invite your body to rest and heal as it sleeps tonight while YOU take a journey of adventure traversing the inner realms through your dreams. When you know that you are dreaming and can have that multi-level consciousness of a lucid dream, just observe and take it all in. Dreams are messages from our unconscious and subconscious bodies, they are subtle and illusive so pay attention as you enter into your dreams ask to be healed and receive the healing.

♥Lift higher into your light tonight and shift your consciousness into your Soul Awareness. Drift, float and journey into greater realms of reality than what's present on this physical Earth. Explore and learn what is available; the blessings are at hand. May the loving light of Spirit bathe you and restore you always as you remember... you are the light.

♥Tonight take time to thank your body, each organ, each part. Bring your appreciation to your physical form and bless it all. Express gratitude for how well your body is working with you for it's your vehicle in this form. Allow the space to open within you, widen your consciousness and expand into new realms. Release your mind as you begin to dream and ride the waves of creativity and balance into deeper places. Anoint yourself with the sacred sounds and light of God, ride this energy into the truth of yourself. Blessings of sweet gentle loving and healing joy for all of you.

♥Bless your body as it sleeps so it is surrounded with healing prayers to regenerate. Ride the light of your dreams throughout the night and discover the reality of your inner worlds and imagination. Bring back keys to your next steps towards your transformation and take daily action to manifest your "dreams come true." Strum the thread of Spirit and resonate with all that is divine and perfect. Baruch Bashan.... gentle blessings at that. Come into harmony and one accord with this loving essence and become the blessing that you already are.

♥While your body heals during sleep allow yourself to drift into your dreams and transcend this level. Explore your Spiritual realms and reconnect with your Soul. Renew yourself on every level that is you, gain insight, lucid awareness and gentle understanding during your inward journey travels in the night. Reconnect and integrate all that you know with all of your new experiences and trust your own unique process. You are blessed, protected and loved beyond measure. Rest well and sleep deeply that's how to care for yourself.

♥Care for yourself in every way by loving who you are; your body, mind, emotions and inner light. As you acknowledge and appreciate yourself, perhaps in the mirror each night, you will open to receive a profound healing. Nurture yourself and grace your Soul with loving kindness tonight as you prepare to be whisked away by your Dream Angel. Visualize what you deserve to have, do and be. Invite your slumber to heal you and your dreams to reveal to you how to attain the life you yearn to live. Be present, that's the real gift and receive the elixir of healing grace.

♥As you lay down to sleep, send loving thoughts and energy to all the parts of your physical body that is out of balance, in pain or strain. Take time to LOVE YOURSELF by healing your body. Allow any negative thoughts or feelings to melt away and focus on pure loving light and Spirit to fill, surround and protect you throughout the night. Bless all that is you and what you're learning. Expand into your Soul, your infinite energy and connect with the Light and Sound of God, plug into the healing grace and receive.

♥Open yourself to receive exactly what you yearn for and deserve while surrounding yourself in the sacred light of healing and renewal as you drift off to dreamland. Declare out loud what you want! Ask for it, and open yourself to receive! Affirm your worthiness and self love to transform yourself into radiant vibrant health and well being. Visualize yourself as you'd like to become and invite your dreams to pave the way to the new you. The deeper you sleep the more you will heal so breathe deeply, releasing it all into the light and dream sweetly this very night.

♥Breathe in this moment and be present, here and now, release everything else. Focus on your own energy to surround your body with healing light as you drift into a deep sleep. Envelop yourself in the amazing journey through your dream realms and explore what is available for you. Relax... Let go, Be light. Allow your dreams to take you safely through the night ...dream sweetly and receive.

♥Tonight, sleep deeply and seek deeper into the depths of your Soul. Pay attention to your unfoldment and keep taking the next step. Maintain your focus for your rainbow is just over the next hill... keep going. Ask to receive, be open to be fulfilled, surrender all that is not for your highest good. Receive the blessings of the night for that is when the light shines brightest.

♥Be MINDFUL of your "self-talk"... FILL your MIND with GOODNESS and your body will respond to match the POSITIVE UPLIFTING thoughts; especially in preparation for a good night's sleep to rest and restore yourself. Energy follows thought, heal your body by healing your thoughts, speak kindly and be good to yourself. As you fill yourself up with goodness your dreams will unravel with grace! Declare what you deserve to enjoy in your life and watch your dreams pave the way.

♥Surrender your body to your bed as you sleep and lift past this level through your dream zone to enter the mystical and magical realms of light and sound. Witness the display of light and images with wonder and purity in lieu of thinking of meaning and purpose. Just be present and give yourself that gift of being in the now. When your consciousness is open and expanded much will be revealed to you. Dream sweetly, dream deeply, dream the whole night through.

♥Be gentle with yourself tonight and appreciate what you've completed and accomplished while taking a breath and nurturing your Soul with gratitude. There is no hurry, no rush, no "have to now" so simply BREATHE and RELAX into the night. Let the moon the stars and the angels embrace you and guide you into your dreams. Be aware of the nuances and the subtle energy that can generate transformation for you and heal you on all levels. ASK so that you may RECEIVE... cuddle up into this evening and know that all is well.

♥Sleep deeply... dream well ...throughout the whole night. Focus on your loving heart and BREATHE in all the goodness. Put your mind at rest and dream sweetly. Allow yourself to receive the gentle transformation of loving as an energetic which heals, restores and creates. Envelop yourself in the magic of the night where dreams are seeds to the possibilities that are waiting for you to receive them.

♥Breathe in the night sky and exhale the past day. Delight in the stars that twinkle brightly. As you drift into your dreams and travel in your body of light, pay attention to your guides, angels and Travelers who are always with you to protect you and awaken your consciousness. Fill and surround yourself in the deepest level of loving gratitude that you are aware of for this is the foundation of healing. Cuddle up in the blanket of gentle loving light which covers you throughout the night and dream the night away.

♥As you close your eyes in the dark of night follow your inner eye to the light within. Be drawn to the clarity, brilliance and truth of your Soul Awareness tonight as you sleep. Dreams are one gateway to this path, spiritual practice is another... whatever your path, partake in it and expand your consciousness into the unknown until it is completely known. Fill surround and protect yourself with this LIGHT so that your journey is filled with joy and grace. BREATHE... breathe... relax and begin your night journey into dreamland.

♥Be light as you enter this night through the dream gate into your self-care and Soul Travel. Breathe in all that you want to receive and flourish with from this moment on. Flow with the rhythm of your life and dance upon the vibrations of your night journey. Be free, be new, discover the authentic you.

♥Be open tonight, as you sleep keep your consciousness open to receive all that is possible through and beyond your dreams. Surrender this physical world to know greater truths that are more real and absolute than your mind can conceive. Listen with your Spiritual heart, see through the eyes of your Soul, and your ears will hear the most heavenly sounds beyond what can be heard on Earth. Keep lifting into the higher realms as you dream gently and sweetly tonight.

♥Heal deeply by resonating with these sacred sounds of the "sound current" and as your body rocks itself to sleep, like a baby in a lullaby, the sonar waves will soothe your body and melt the pain away. Listen for the sound deep within your dreams, and let it lead you to healing grace. Dream sweetly and awake in the morning a new and wonderful you!

♥Sustain yourself tonight with your deep breathing as you relax enough to fall asleep. With each breath invite your body to heal itself as it restores every cell during the night. Unfold your consciousness to expand into the etheric realms through the threads of your dreams. Weave in and out, over and around all the symbols, fragments of thoughts, pieces of memory as your dreams integrate all of this into a form of communication. Surrender to a higher power, your inner master, the wisdom of your Soul and keep unfolding while you simply keep breathing, sleeping and dreaming.

♥Radiant light bathe us tonight to our Soul's delight, so we may transcend into the highest realms while we dream. Surrender this day and this world to enter the zone of Spiritual awakening while your body sleeps deeply and restores itself. Remember the images, symbols, colors and sounds that will add to your joy and fulfillment, for that's what dreams are made of. Wrap yourself in the sacred light and sleep tight.

♥Prepare for your dreams by focusing in the center of your peaceful heart tonight as you let the day fall away. Breathe in the gentle night and calm yourself on all levels. From this center of clarity and stillness you will begin your dream time and travel into deeper levels of your consciousness. Simply take notice to what you see and what you hear. For the dream visions in the night whisper our future to us in miraculous ways. Each dream brings you closer to your Soul in the process of healing.

♥Caress your body with gratitude as you lay down to sleep. Relax and surrender into your dreams with ease and grace. Let your thoughts fly away like busy butterflies so your mind is open and clear ...and so your dreams begin. Open to receive a beginning of healing and renewal for your dreams will lead the way.

♥Center yourself in your heart tonight as you place your body at rest for a deep and healing sleep. Focus on your heartbeat and follow that rhythm into your dreams like a distant drum beating with cadence and harmony. It's beckoning you with every beat. Observe how the sound of your heartbeat transforms into music then into light. Follow the rays of light and sound into deeper dream realms. Reach into the core of your being. Know that this sound and light is from the very essence of you, whispering exactly what you yearn to hear. Follow your dreams on every level and love yourself completely.

♥Hush your thoughts and take in a deep breath to let this day fall away so your body will be at ease and fall asleep. Stir your Soul so you can ride the energy of light into your dreams. In the quite of this peace listen for the deeper sound within your Soul and follow this sacred music high into the Spiritual realms. Renew yourself and embrace radiant health and balance as you anoint yourself with the sound and light which is present. Dreams can be subtle and peaceful, so expand into whatever shows up and dream the night away.

♥Sleep deeply and rest your mind so you can freely enter your dream tunnel. Focus on your breathing and heighten your senses to take it all in for each dream has keys for us all. Float in and out of dream reality by remaining present in the now and be willing to receive the gifts that await you. Pay attention and stay awake in your dreams as you continue to sleep and observe perfection.

♥Refresh yourself tonight as you bask in the radiant divine light. Nourish your Soul in the sacred waters as you drink from the well of Spirit. Within each dream is a key for you but you must recognize that key so stay awake while you dream. Dreams are ribbons that weave through our consciousness to reveal what we are solving, resolving and receiving. Quench your thirst and revel in the wisdom each dream offers you.

♥Jettison yourself into your dreams tonight with intention and focus. Embrace the darkness until the light beacon welcomes you to the other side. The deeper your journey the greater the gifts of wisdom so keep moving further into the esoteric realms. Lucid clarity will appear when your consciousness is ready to understand... it's a process. Revel in the sacred unfoldment of remembering who you are as each aspect is revealed as you Soul Travel the night through.

♥Transcend this world tonight by leaving your form behind, your body to rest while you travel the inner realms. Increase your awareness of the essence which you are within your body and beyond your body. Extend your essence beyond your thoughts beyond this physical world, keep reaching and stretching further. You are lighter than air and brighter than the sun. Formless essence is who you truly are which is brilliant, divine and holy.

"If you can cultivate wholesome mental states prior to sleep and allow them to continue right into sleep without getting distracted, then sleep itself becomes wholesome." ~**Dalai Lama**

Judith Ternyik

Relaxation & Stress Relief

One of the greatest challenges for so many is the ability to enjoy a good solid night's sleep. It's hard to relax when you're so wound up with stress and tension. That level of anxiety produces a "fight/flight" response and the adrenalin pumps through our body making it nearly impossible to fall asleep.

These nightly blessings will guide your awareness and consciously move your focus through specific methods to induce relaxation and release of tension. When stress is managed and transformed we create a state of homeostasis and our body is able to heal. Let go, release your stress, and surrender to the relaxed state of being that you deserve to enjoy.

"You have no need to travel anywhere. Journey within yourself, enter a mine of rubies and bathe in the splendor of your own light."
~Rumi

♥R E L A X with your breath tonight ...slowly breathe deeply and gently release fully. Empty your mind with the day to prepare for your night travel. Focus on the memories and thoughts which bring you to a deeper place of sacred peaceful calm. Bless your body and bring loving attention to any place that hurts by simply visualizing bright sacred light bathing that space. Let go ...release ...relax, your dreams are waiting for you.

♥Let your dreams take you into the night so relax deeply and breathe fully as you drift off to sleep. Follow your stream of dreams through all the adventures on the inner levels. Soul travel into the highest light as you surrender the day to gain perspective and insight. Dream sweetly and rest well as you let your breath rise and fall with deeper relaxation.

♥Lay down the day to sleep and your body to renew with a relaxing rest through the night. Elevate your awareness and transform through the levels to know the worlds without end. Meet the Angels who are always with you, is it a dream, it matters not, just keep lifting higher. Like the caterpillar who becomes a butterfly we are all evolving and the sooner we let go of trying to figure it out and just flow with the process the greater the possibility of an expansive transformation. Breathe deeply and float into your dreams with wonder and awe as you feel the stress melt away.

♥Quiet yourself tonight, deafen the noise around you, create a peaceful serene space for yourself. As you begin to fall asleep let your mind wonder so your Spirit can wander and gravitate to the light within. Shower yourself with a peaceful calm and slip into your dream-mobile to transport you into alternate consciousness with ease and grace. Enjoy the ride as you discover and explore the MORE available to you as you listen to the silence until you hear the sound form and follow that sacred sound within to a deeper state of wisdom. Dream, dream… dream.

♥RELAX as you close your eyes tonight let your eyes sink deeply into their sockets, allow your body to become heavy and weighted into your bed to anchor your body here. Release your Spirit, your Soul to travel into the light filled realms of wisdom and discovery. As your body relaxes more, realize that NO THING is impossible unless you believe it to be so... open your mind and let it go let it flow into the know. Be present and give yourself the gift of NOW. Rebirth yourself each day with the dreams of what may become each night ...it's all FOR YOU. Claim it, it's yours.

♥Let the gentle waves of relaxation bathe you with total rest tonight and renew your body, mind and Spirit. Allow your mind to relax and drift into the dream state so you can rev up your vibration of light. Become the ONE who transforms into a greater being, be the ONE to contribute to the shift humanity so deserves. We all are blessed beyond our realization, just breathe it in, relax and be with that blessing to enjoy your deep sleep tonight for your dreams will awaken your Soul.

♥Feeling the PRESSURE? Maybe you just "gotta" cook some more??? A diamond would still be a piece of coal without pressure and stress. BREATHE in deeply and let the pressure transform YOU! Blessings of nocturnal bliss as you renew and Soul travel the night through and around each magical dream you have. Relax, let go, it's time for the dream show.

♥Be the light that you already are until you burn the stress from your being. Become more radiant each day glowing with the sacred divine light that you already are. Allow your true self to shine through for all to see. The light will eliminate the dark and eventually the shadows too. When the darkness of this world clouds your perception, turn inward to your own radiant illumination and light up your presence with your own Spirit. Blessings to you all with soft waves of relaxation and restoration tonight as you sleep as each breath and sigh relaxes you even more. Now dream and renew yourself in the sacred light. Breathe in the goodness and rest well, transformation is at hand.

♥Close your eyes and see the darkness until you see the colors of the light peeking through. Take a deep breath of peaceful relaxation to prepare for your dream vision. Just observe each dream, image and symbol... they are all keys to unlock the esoteric aspects of you. Allow the vibrant colors you see in your night journey to bathe your body in a complete healing relaxation and open more discoveries for your awakening consciousness as you dream within your dreams.

♥Sleep well tonight and allow your imagination to wander past the void into the light here is the place you will sink into a stress free sleep. Keep your focus on learning and knowing as you enter the dream zone and relax into your sleep even more. Ask to receive, open yourself to align with your Soul Awareness and live an integrated life. Discover the natural state of your being which is pure joy in a relaxed state. Dreams are mysteries that lay just beyond your knowing and beyond your beliefs. There is much to gain in the process of surrender for it is the process of letting go that we receive. Blessings of harmony and joy tonight and always.

♥OPEN your heart OPEN your mind OPEN your awareness to expand into the majesty of what is already present. BREATHE deeply, RELAX fully, SURRENDER completely tonight as you sleep, restore and follow your dreams deeply into the dark of night. Invite your Soul to awaken to the truth of who you truly are... allow that realization to transform you on all levels. You are precious, valued, significant and a gift to all of humanity. Now take that all in with each breath, own it and begin your dream sojourn.

♥Relax with each breath tonight, allow your body to let go and sink into sleep. Breathe in relaxing rhythms so your mind and emotions surrender to your Soul. Feel the vibration of your breath and heart beat as it lulls you into a lullaby sleep. Begin your dreams sweetly and gently as you travel through the esoteric realms. Nourish your Soul with adventures of greater conscious awakening with every dream in every moment.

♥Breathe deeply to relax your body and with each exhale melt deeper into the night. Align your energy fields into one accord as you expand into the brightest light. Listen inwardly for the vibration of the sound that resonates throughout all time and space. Ascend into your Soul to elevate your awareness into the sweetness of peace as if you are floating with your essence completely open and relaxed. Like the gentle kiss of snowflakes on your skin, let Spirit embrace you tonight. Sleep well and dream sweetly with each gentle breath

♥Take in a deep breath through the center of your heart and expand that fullness throughout your body ...relax as you empty your breath. Welcome your restful slumber with lucid dreams that offer gems of awakening and awareness for you. Traverse the realms of light with wonder and grace as each dream weaves your tapestry. Float gently towards your dreamscape with wonder and ease as you float on each inhale and exhale you will relax even more and journey even deeper.

♥Invite the busy buzzing of your mind, emotions and things of this level to fade away as you focus on your breathing and invite yourself to let go, release and relax. Follow your breath into the beating rhythm of your heart and deepen your relaxation even more. Slip into your dream state as your unconscious mind creates the masterpiece of your dream puzzle tonight with a myriad of symbols. Rest, relax and restore while your Soul travels in the light throughout this night.

♥Rest your eye lids gently as you take in a deep relaxing breath to begin your sleep journey tonight. Sink into your bed with comfort and ease and allow your body to completely relax. Open your inner eye to begin traversing the worlds without end during your dream voyage. Watch the miracles appear which are all designed just for you and keep releasing as you dream the night away.

♥Peacefully fold into yourself to go deep into the center of your core and ignite the streams of your light filled consciousness to envelop your dreams. Focus on your gentle breathing and fill yourself with renewal and healing with each breath. Open your inner eye and observe your journey within as your creativity flourishes and your Soul is nourished with divine knowledge. Peacefully drift into your dream gate and enjoy your unfoldment as you awaken more in each moment with each dream.

♥Ascend into the ethers of light and sound as you open to receive your dreams in the most relaxed state of flotation. Keep lifting higher throughout your dream adventures. As you expand to become the light and the sound becomes you the mystery schools will welcome you. From these esoteric mystical realms there is rich wisdom to learn. Wisdom is knowledge through the heart and you are the truth, the light and the way.

♥Breathe in deeply and sustain that fullness for a while. Let your breath escape with a "shhhhh" sound gently through your lips. Affirm that life is a flowing of energy inward and outward, giving and receiving. Continue with the deep breathing and shhhhh release until you relax DEEPLY into your sleep tonight. Let your body become weighted and heavy as your Soul ascends into the light and begins your dream journey. Quietly relax and receive all that you deserve, and even more than you can imagine.

♥Become a present state of being as you release this day and close your eyes to sleep. Breathe in relaxation and calm your body, mind and feelings to attain a restful state of being. Let your inner light shine bright through the darkness of the night and light up all the possibilities in your dreams. Let your imagination sparkle with wonder as your dreams lead the way to new discoveries. Have an "ah-ha" night of sweet dreams as you illuminate your consciousness and relax your body.

♥Relax tonight before you close your eyes, gaze at something that puts your mind at rest, empty your thoughts and feelings before you lay back and close your eyes. Listen to soft music with simple sounds or nature sounds and take in the peace from your ears. From this place of peaceful emptiness, you can fill the void with possibilities of wonder and joy. Be swept away by your dreams into a myriad of symbols and images which will leave clues for you to follow. Be carried into the light as you Soul travel the night and breathe deeply of the peaceful presence.

♥Fold your body into your bed and into the night as you relax and breathe in the quiet. Look deeply into the void until you begin to see the distortions and images which will transport you into your dreamland. Observe your journey into the inner worlds without end and pay attention to what is revealed to you for every dream is a gem. Bring yourself into the light, restore yourself in every way, release to receive and dream on. Allow yourself to enjoy the most deeply relaxing sleep of your life.

♥Dream time beckons you to relax and drift to off to sleep. Breathe in the sacred peace and inner light that glows within you. Reflect on the beauty present around you, even when you look in the mirror, especially when you look in the mirror. Lay your body down to rest and close your eyes to enter a deep healing sleep. Ride your dreams into the void of wisdom and glean inner knowledge to set your sails to higher ground while your stress fades away.

♥Envelop your body in a cocoon of light tonight to relax and bless each part of your physical body. Breathe deeply and surrender into your deep peaceful sleep and into your dream escape towards the ethers beyond this realm and traverse the worlds without end. Pay attention to the images and symbols shown to you and let them illuminate your path as you put the pieces together for each dream is a gem of discovery.

♥Close your eyes, relax into the night and breathe in the sacred breath of peace. Extend your awareness into the source that you are and renew yourself. Let your body melt into a healing pool of restoration as your Soul ascends into the light of dream realms. Become the light as you expand into the esoteric realms of mystical magical wonders through each dream. Release, Relax, Renew.

♥Anoint yourself with the sacred waters of divine light as you imagine yourself surrendering and falling into grace. Breathe deeply of the renewal in each breath and gently sink into your restful sleep. Traverse the mystical inner worlds without end to unravel your consciousness as you awaken each aspect in perfect timing. Dreams are the gateway into self-realization so realize the potential that is within you and let go and reveal your authentic true self with each dream, in each moment

♥Surrender to your Soul through the purest essence of who you are as you allow your dreams to wisk you away into the ethers and beyond this world. While you sleep deeply through the night your dreams will relax you completely. Transform and travel through esoteric dimensions of space and time and give your dreams permission to awaken you more on each level. Rest your body, empty your mind, calm your emotions and delve into your dreams.

♥Release all your energies into Mother Earth and relax completely into your sleep zone tonight. Surrender all your pain, thoughts and feelings to be completely free as you weave your way into your dreams. Allow your body to bask in the light and heal as you Soul Travel this night journey into worlds without end within every dream.

♥Take in a deep breath… and sustain it in your lungs to relax you at deeper levels… now gently exhale with a releasing sound. Let your body sink deeply into your bed and gently put your mind and emotions to rest as you float into your sleep. Begin your dream journey with total trust as your Soul travels the night weaving through each dream in divine perfection. Sleep, dream, heal.

♥Let your mind flow like a stream as your head rests on your pillow tonight and you slip into a deep relaxing sleep. Allow your dreams to unravel all your feelings and thoughts into the images of "dream talk" and observe as the magic unfolds. Dreams are very healing so relax, release, and recover while you sleep the night away.

♥Surrender deeply to relax as you expand your body fully. Breathe deeply and sustain that breath until the tension releases... exhale and relax. Visualize your body restoring itself as it heals while you sleep so you can leave your body behind and begin your night journey through your dreams. As you float and ride upon the sound current you may reach the cosmic mirror and see yourself in the reflection. Let your dreams take you into where you need to go, let go and trust your process. Bathe your Soul in light and journey deeper.

"Let gratitude be the pillow upon which you kneel to say your nightly prayer. And let faith be the bridge you build to overcome evil and welcome good." ~**Maya Angelou**

Judith Ternyik

Relationships & Relating

Many people yearn for a "relationship" to enjoy the company of another person to share and care with. Relationships take many forms from our parents, siblings, spouses, colleagues, neighbors to actually even our own selves. Often people define a relationship as a person to person, yet relationships are all encompassing. How you relate to the family pet, your bank account, dealing with laundry all represent a aspects of a relationship.

By becoming aware of what your patterns are you will gain insight about your own relationships with the world around you. When you learn how to relate to yourself you may understand how that reflects on your relationships with other people and circumstances in your world. The dream blessings in this book will guide you to increase your awareness and prepare you to attract the qualities you seek in all your relationships.

"How you relate to the issue is the issue. You may or may not have ever thought about this, but one of the deepest yearnings of people everywhere, is the longing to be truly heard. Surely, nowhere is this need more keenly experienced than in close personal relationships. One reason friendships often last longer than love affairs and marriages is that friends truly love being together and listening to each other." **~Drs. Ron and Mary Hulnick**

♥Leave your body behind to heal and rest as you pass through the gate to another reality while you deepen into your sleep and listen to yourself. Float and drift into your dreams for they will transport you into discoveries and journeys that may enlighten you in many ways. Consider what you'd like more of or how to better a relationship with another or perhaps yourself. Observe and transform all that you decide to take in and take on and remember You are divine light, a precious Soul, learning and growing into all that you are.

♥Champion yourself tonight as you tuck your inner child into bed! Every relationship "out there" is a reflection of your relationship with yourself. Acknowledge the best people in your circle of life in your prayers and know that you will become the very best YOU possible! There is a child, a "basic self" in all of us. What has your Inner Child learned today? Sharing is caring so love yourself to sleep and dream of goodness tonight. As you love yourself more you will attract more loving relationships into your life.

♥Tonight, in your prayers, speak into existence what you deserve to have, be and enjoy. Declare your intentions and desires and place that into the LIGHT and pay attention to your dreams and inner wisdom. Traverse the inner worlds without end as you slip into and over the sheathe of light and glimmer more wisdom with each dream. Sleep well, rest completely and awake renewed tomorrow.

♥As our eye lids close tonight to dream the night away... let's all connect with our LIGHT, our real self which transcends this physical realm. Release the form and float into the formless as a discovery into a greater reality more authentic than the mind can realize. BE THE LIGHT that you already are... for this energetic will allow such a deep transformation on all levels, you will awaken as if reborn anew. The more you integrate yourself the greater partner you will be for another. Time to sleep, dream and create.

♥As I lay me down to sleep, I reconnect, plug in my Spiritual Light with God's light and re-member myself to all that is God's creation. Like the Aspen and the Weeping Willow Trees which are all connected through their roots and energy; "We are all one" within the Spiritual Light. LOVE YOURSELF TO SLEEP TONIGHT... give your worries and concerns over to "our father" and set yourself free to traverse and transform your most magnificent dream into reality here and now. Open yourself to manifest what you desire as you too become that very desire with yourself.

♥BREATHE DEEPLY and Relax your body and leave it to rest while your Soul journey begins as you dream on and through the dimensions. We're all connected by threads of light and sound vibrations so relax into your night dreams, journey with discovery and awe. You will attract to you what energy vibe you resonate with. Become what you seek and let your dreams guide your way. Everything you see and experience is FOR YOU so partake and be joyful. You are blessed... trust, surrender and dive into your dreams.

♥Drop your thoughts, feelings and even your body …let them all rest tonight while you go on your DREAM JOURNEY. Dream of what you want to create in your life, the quality of relationships you deserve to enjoy. Detach your essence by using your imagination to mock up the perfect state of being… breathe in deeply as you drift into sleep and into your dream world. This journey is real yet subtle, pay attention and return in the morning with keys to transform your life here on Earth and attract the perfect partner for you.

♥Tonight as you prepare for your restful dreams ask for what you want and be open to receive. Let go of the struggles of this world and open to reconnect your essence of light to that which is filled with light, loving and peace. Receive the blessings and be transported into other dimensions of yourself through your dream state. Become like a column of light anchored and grounded yet extending ever upward reaching for more grace and excellence... Ride the current of sacred sound and light into the depth of all truth as you dream this night away. You may be surprised who notices you differently in the morning.

♥Give yourself the gift of receiving a peaceful sleep tonight. Let your mind stream and empty and your emotions drift away. The light you hold in the palm of your hands will be the miracles you pray for when you learn how to direct this sacred light for the highest good. Ask the question and receive the answer... pay close attention to your dreams they are the gateway to treasures yet discovered. Shhhh... shhh... listen, breathe and listen more... to prepare; for what you seek is also seeking you.

♥Tonight, as you prepare for sleep, be childlike. Be present in the now, innocent, pure with a sense of wonderment. Breathe deeply of the grace and renewal to fill your body with awareness and health ...release your breath and send it all around the world to bless all who will breathe in the same air as you. Be still and cuddle up to your peaceful center as you drift off to sleep and slip into your wonderful land of dreamy dreams of the perfect relationship you deserve to have with every person in your circle.

♥Rest well tonight as you enter your dreamscape and journey, like a shooting star, gathering all the wishes of many who yearn. Dream your own dream while sleeping and awake, open your consciousness and stretch your vision even more. Know that you deserve to receive your deepest wish... attract that to you by invitation and being open to receive. Surrender to receive, trust and believe, know that this time is for you. Your dreams are waiting.

♥Tonight TRANSFORM yourself as you travel through your dream gate. Become the essence of light that you already are. Leave your body behind to rest and restore while you traverse the inner realms of light, sound and Spirit. YOU hold the keys to your awakening... WAKE UP while you sleep. Transform into the relationship you yearn for and be that person that you seek in another. Remember and reconnect to your source, that which is, towards your own realization of your authentic self. Soul travel the night away as you sleep deeply and dream sweetly.

♥Reach past your imagination tonight to take a quantum leap beyond your dreams. Travel the "dream worm hole" to the far reaches of your consciousness where silence has a gentle sound and colors are vibrating with intensity and perfection. See with your inner eye and know with your Spirit that this journey is your Soul passage your own awakening. Observe your current life situation and see how you can bring forward greater joy and companionship for yourself in this vivid dream state. Wake up as you sleep... the world is waiting for you.

♥Welcome the night when we cannot see with our eyes... we have the opportunity to use our inner vision to see beyond what we have perceived. Take the leap of faith, and focus inward to your inner knowing, your Soul Awareness, and take a look from that perspective. Insight is IN SIGHT... so look within and see what's been missing. Jump on a dream wave and ride it through to greater wisdom and allow it to reveal answers that you have yet to ask. Behold a new beginning and begin it now and fill in the void with your own realization dream by dream.

♥Sleep deeply and breathe fully while you also maintain your awareness during your dreams. When our mind and emotions are resting our consciousness is more open to receive the perfection and direction from divine realms. Tune into the esoteric mystical levels where dreams are created and bring back the pieces needed to put your puzzle together. Send your energy up and out to call forward into your life what you think is missing, place yourself out as a blessing for another. Watch your dreams come true.

♥Move toward the loving energetic of your heart tonight as you detach yourself from the things and concerns of this world. Elevate your awareness as you ascend into the light and begin your dream journey. Access your higher power of wisdom and gain insight and perspective with a multilevel consciousness of loving awareness. When the door opens will you have the courage to walk though? Imagine who you would like to walk through those doors with you. Someone else just may be sharing your dream with you!

♥Lay your body down to rest, relax and recover while you ascend in your body of light to prepare for a convergence. Hush your thoughts and calm your feelings so you can travel freely within your Soul to the highest realms. Dreams are often the vehicle to explore these esoteric levels... so dream the night away. Pay attention, there are many pieces of the puzzle presented to you within each dream. Lay the foundation of what you deserve to have and share as you let your dreams set the stage for receiving. Pay close attention to who is receiving you!

♥Let your dreams transport you to freedom through the process of trust. All that is you, is all FOR YOU, nothing is against you so dive into your dreams now. These subtle energies can be mysterious, even mystical, trust your process and dream on. As you deepen your trust in yourself you will radiate integrity into the world and attract the relationships you can trust. The first person you must trust... is yourself.

♥Converge and awaken to the truth of who you are within each dream to set yourself free. Through the tunnels of dreams into the hallways of symbols and pieces of images ALL will lead you a place of sacred wisdom ...your own center, your Soul. Keep lifting higher and deeper into the light within and stay there a while. Invite your precious loved ones into your sacred light and anoint each with blessings galore. Give yourself a gift and simply be present, unfold and transform beyond each dream.

♥Leave your body to sleep and rest while you transcend into your dreams. Transform into the light that you are and Soul travel as you weave your way threading each dream into a tapestry of awareness. As you increase your sensitivity to these subtle levels new visas of majesty will open to you. Sleep well and journey far forget all that you know to discover greater truths. Everything in your life is a relationship within your own being.

♥Let yourself transform from your body into your essence of light. Leave your body to sleep, rest and restore while you ascend this realm and delve into the inner worlds of dream weaving. Observe the patterns of light; perhaps some faces and places you know and continue to be neutral and open in your consciousness. Each dream is a piece of the puzzle and when you're ready to know, the pieces will fall into place. Value your self-worth, affirm that you deserve to enjoy the life you imagine, now off to your dreams to make them come true.

♥Journey deeply into your dreams and discover the mystical mysteries to be revealed. Feel the pulse of life vibrating though your consciousness with every breath and relax into this dream moment. Become open as you flow like water into deeper dreams to realize that all relationships reveal aspects of how you are with yourself. Ramp up your self-love to fill yourself completely and you will positively affect everyone in your life that you relate to. Vibrate with the light and sound to attract those to you of which you dream of.

♥Release this day and the past as you empty yourself for a peaceful deeply restful sleep. Should you shed a tear of tenderness, gratitude or longing consider that your own tear anoints you with a blessing of transformation and healing. Bathe yourself in the sacred light as you breathe deeply of the nurturing comfort that is present. Bask in the dark of night and drift into your dreams with freedom and awe to learn more of the mysteries within yourself. You are a journey worth taking and developing a relationship with yourself first is the key to unlock your treasures.

♥Nocturnal blessings for you... open your mind and your heart to expand your consciousness into knowing what is within you... mysteries of the universe and beyond are within YOU. The wisdom you seek is within your reach so jump into your dream adventure and explore the possibilities available for you. The deeper you go the more you'll know... journey to the essence of being deep within yourself! And love, love, love yourself completely.

♥Breathe in deeply and release with a sigh...ahh. Relax into your sleep and invite your body, mind and emotions to restore and heal on all levels. Ascend into your light and float into your essence as you begin your dream journey tonight. Be here and there and aware of it all through your lucid dreaming and Soul travel. On the other side of each dream is your dream come true so just keep breathing and declare it for yourself.

♥Invite the night to sweep you away into the deepest recesses of your Soul as you journey through your dreams. Engage and surrender so you remain ever present in the NOW. Release to receive and ride your dreams with greater awareness into the deepest knowing possible for yourself. Notice who is noticing you in your dreams and when you're awake! NOW is the only real time. You are attracting exactly what you deserve to enjoy into your life.

♥Breathe in the LIGHT and be transformed as you ascend into the realm of dreams. Listen to the sounds with messages just for you. Look with curious eyes to see the images that will redirect your focus. It's all custom created just for you so you can have the quality of relationships and life you deserve to enjoy. Pay close attention as your dreams decode the mystery of what you seek and deserve to have. Affirm your worthiness to receive your desires.

♥Set your focus for what you'd like to receive from your dream travel, the answers you seek, the direction or clarity you'd like... and let that focus become your pathway. Open your awareness as you learn and experience altered states of consciousness during your night travels in your body of light, the purity of your Soul, the true essence of who you really are. Your Soul flight will take you to the places and faces you yearn to know. Keep breathing and dreaming, the best is yet to come. Dreams do come true.

♥Take in a long deep breath then exhale your breath completely with a sacred sound and listen to the sound deep within your Soul. The song of the Divine is always present within you. Listen for the harmony and healing vibration as you gently fall asleep. Listen for your inner song and let the music move you and harmonize with others of the same resonating sound. Rest well and restore yourself with each and every dream. Allow the sacred sound to attract to you as your future unfolds.

♥Let go of this world as you prepare to sleep, dream and heal. Embrace the worlds without end within yourself and let your dreams unfold like the petals of a flower. Plant the seed of transformation and cultivate your process with loving care, now invite relationships to enter into your life to enjoy the abundance together. Always be willing to renew yourself with each breath to give yourself the gift of being present.

♥Find your sacred center and breathe in peace as you become still. Be aware of the quiet sound and gentle vibration in that is inside this stillness. Anchor your awareness to this source, this divine light and surrender to your sleep. Float away into your dreams to receive their blessing of sorting and balancing all unresolved issues and concerns. You're in the "dream zone" and from this state of freedom and relaxation you can balance yourself completely and fully on every level, release your past and welcome the future you dream of.

"In a dream, in a vision of the night, while slumbering on their beds, then He opens the ears of men, and seals their instruction."
~ **Book of Job (33: 15-16)**

Judith Ternyik

Passion & Purpose

Are you living on purpose? Is your life and are your goals on purpose? We may start out with a big picture of what we want for our life usually with enthusiasm and passion but over the years, things often change. As life gets in the way of our purpose we may lose our gusto and our passion. Often the mundane will creep in and one day fades into the next until we feel like lifeless zombies.

Taking the time to reignite your passion as you redefine your purpose will propel you into your life with energy and enthusiasm. When we know we are on track we feel a sense of success and accomplishment which feeds our passion! This collection of dream blessings is intended to facilitate your process of becoming clear with your purpose and identifying what you are passionate about. As you track your dreams you may discover a whole new way of living your life with passion and purpose. Living a live "on purpose" ignites our passion!

"When you catch a glimpse of your potential, that's when passion is born." ~**Zig Ziglar**

♥Set yourself free and DREAM BIG, really, REALLY big. Acknowledge what stirs your Soul, what you would spend time doing if there were no concerns or demands on you. Dream freely and follow your intuition to each next step as your dreams lay it out for you. EVERYTHING IS FOR YOU, make sure you're not against yourself! SLEEP, DREAM, REST, RECOVER, HEAL and become the miracle you dream of.

♥Tonight, plant your seed, your wish, your dream as you drift off to sleep. Hold your vision and infuse it with your emotional enthusiasm and your sacred passion, while at the same time, be detached too. Let your dreams carry this seed into the light of Spirit, into Heaven, where it can grow and prosper and then... return to you here! Share your gratitude for all that you enjoy and honor... release your thoughts and feelings as you empty yourself to have a solid healing sleep. Your seed will be nurtured and nourished, remember what you can from each dream tonight... for it is a key to living your dream life!

♥Your "self-talk" is your inner prayer... what are you telling the universe tonight? Let the chaos of others and our world spin outside of your sphere and breathe into your peace as you center yourself. Turn down the volume in your head and focus into your meditation and prayer as you prepare for sleepy dream time. Place into your energy what you love the most, what you are passionate about and let your dreams clarify your purpose.

♥Sleep well, dream deeply and discover more about you than you'll ever realize awake. Life comes into focus a bit at a time. Breathe in fully all the goodness you can receive and release the old with each exhale. Renew yourself with each breath and the LIGHT of SPIRIT as you enjoy your journey on this path called life. Embrace the unique gifts you have to offer and share, then take this into your sleep and into your dreams to ignite them with greater passion.

♥Prepare for a deep, restful, peaceful healing sleep tonight. Breathe in all goodness and gently let this day fall away as you focus on your purpose here. Visualize our Earth and all living things thriving with radiant health and balance. Send forth your light and energy to seed the change for our "New Earth" to emerge and for the authentic you to arrive. Ask your dreams to clarify your passion and purpose so you can bring forth your gifts into this world. It is your divine heritage.

♥Be smart. Be aware. Be conscious. Become what you deserve, what you actually already are. BE for a while instead of "doing" and BE mindful of your own self talk, even your thoughts... program what you DESERVE to enjoy in your life. Your passion is your foundation! As you fall into slumber review your day, and delete any negative judgments, change the channel when you realize the "blah, blah, blah" stinking thinking. TALK & THINK GOOD STUFF and you will attract GOOD STUFF into your world. Dive into your dreams with purpose and intention.

♥Sink deeply into your slumber tonight. Wrap yourself in the warmth of your cozy blankets and the brilliant light of your Soul as you reconnect with your passion. Ride the silk waves of Spirit into the night and weave your way through your dreams. Awaken the deepest part of your consciousness to greater awareness of why you are here, who you are and what you are to become to live your life with passion. BEGIN NOW, and open your mind, heart and Soul to embrace the blessings and dreams that await your acknowledgement.

♥Inhale the sacredness of this night as you exhale the past completely. Become present in the now and drift into your relaxed sleep to drift further into your dream portal and begin your journey. Float among the stars and shapes of colors that surround you while your dreams stream into worlds without end. From this abstract perspective you will gain new insight and awareness to truths that have gone unnoticed or forgotten. Open your heart, open your Spiritual eyes and ears and travel a sacred path to knowing your passion with each breath you take. Dig deeper to discover a greater purpose for your life.

♥What will you offer yourself this evening as you prepare to enter the dream state? How will you open to the possibilities of transforming your form to the formless? Only when you give to your own self, let go of beliefs that may hold you from growing can you then truly experience a quantum shift. Passionately transcend tonight and become fully the radiant light of your being so you can traverse the worlds without end into new depths and journeys your Soul yearns for. You are the blessing!

♥IT WILL BE if and only if YOU DECLARE IT SO! Say what you deserve to have and enjoy, DECLARE what you will create and manifest in your life. Energy follows thought and words create intention and doing creates action. DO IT, say it, become it Then leave the rest to your sweet dreams tonight! That's how to fan the flames of your passion and purpose.

♥Open to a revealing sleep tonight and invite the esoteric dreams into your awareness. Breathe deeply and send that breath to all the places in your body that hurt or are stuck... ask "what is my purpose now" and listen. Allow your Soul to travel and traverse the inner realms to open your conscious mind and your Spiritual Awareness where your passion was born. Feel, embrace and know the blessings abound are waiting for you to receive. Loving surrounds you always. Dream with gusto and go for it when you're awake!

♥Take your dream journey all the way tonight into the realms of symbols to worlds without end. Soul travel with the light and sound of Spirit and bask in the renewal and peace which is always present. Devour your demons and worries with the courage of your loving heart and purity of your spirit... TRANSFORM ...you deserve the best of everything! Dream in full color with passion.

♥Close your eyes and see the darkness become a brilliant light show ...prepare for your dreams as you surrender the day and release your worries. Breathe deeply from the core of your center and be aware of the pendulum of balance which is never still yet continues to move within you. Passions may change over your life time, take time to redefine it now. Drift deeper into your consciousness and let the light that you are balance, renew and invigorate what you most love to experience. Travel further to open your awareness to all the blessings waiting for you to receive fully.

♥When you lay down to sleep... BREATHE DEEPLY ...and surrender your Soul into the night... invite your body to float, rest and heal. As you let the day fade away you will expand your awareness and consciousness into a more vivid realm of reality just beyond your dream state. Flow with the energy and light... this is your life, your journey of discovery into your purpose for this life. Ask and receive... dream and believe... your success is yours to achieve.

♥Move past the illusions of this physical world tonight as you sleep deeply and dream magnificently. Reach past what appears to be fixed and into the sacred mystical esoteric realms of living light. Explore the many levels of your awareness until you become conscious of all realities and know your Soul intimately. Where your passion lives is where the answers are waiting for you. Caress your body in the gentle light tonight, transform your being into your higher frequency of vibrational pure radiant light. Now go light up your world with your passionate purpose.

♥Set your dream intention tonight as you enter the gate into esoteric travels while your body sleeps deeply through the night. Ask your question to know a greater purpose so the answer can be revealed to you in symbols and meaning your subconscious understands. Your dream journey is an awakening of the greater part of yourself so enjoy the discovery and adventure of this fantastic sojourn and remember that passion can be like a gentle breeze of peaceful calm.

♥Keep going deeper into your dreams there is so much there for you to know. Just continue onward and notice it all as your dreams reveal so much for your awareness. Enjoy the ride, the journey, the trek ...as you remember what is deep within your being. You will also remember how to integrate yourself with your greater consciousness and align your passion with this life. Dreams are the vehicle into the greater depths of our Soul to reveal the hidden places of who we truly are. Sleep, dream, discover... and grow.

♥Align yourself tonight with the sacred light within your Soul and ride that current of energy into your dreams. Ascend this physical level and expand to the subtle energy of light and sound so you can follow your own vibration and passion into the void of possibilities. Let go of all that no longer serves you to open to receive what will support you in your next steps. Set your intention and pay attention to what is revealed to you in your dreams.

♥Gently close your eyes and breathe deeply and slowly as you gaze inwardly into the dark. Through the layers of darkness light will begin to appear, always follow the light. Let the dark of the night envelop you in comfort and rest while you begin your inner journey through your tunnel of dreams. Enter the mystery schools of esoteric knowledge with awareness through the understanding of your dreams and the core of your purpose. Nourish yourself with this divine sacred wisdom each dream offers you.

♥Lay your head down and rest your body as you breathe deeply and relax some more. Detach your mind from thinking about what you're passionate about and let yourself drift through the veil of dreamland to the other side. Observe the images and symbols that float by as you release your Soul to travel the inner realms. Journey into altered states through the overlapping dimensions to gain insight and wisdom beyond this level. The more open you are the more you will receive so open wide to take it all in.

♥Release this day and prepare for this night with deep breaths of gratitude and relaxation. Lift past this level of illusions, this world and worries into and through the cosmic mirror towards the worlds without end through your dream threads. What you see is also seeing you so look closely and discover the keys to your freedom, the depth of your passion and how to live your life on purpose. Dream sweetly and deeply and gather the many "ah-ha's" in remembering and reconnecting through all the veils of consciousness.

♥Time to tune into our Soul and inner light as we prepare for a restful sleep tonight. Rev up your vibration with gratitude and sacred meditation so your body will restore while you ascend into your dreams. Flicker with the light which surrounds you and float into the mystery schools from dream to dream. Sleep deeply and have wondrous dreams as you Soul Travel with passion and glory.

♥Enter your dream zone by surrendering all of your worldly concerns tonight and let this day fall away as you gently breathe yourself into a deep sleep. Swim into the sacred waters through your dreams into the awareness of your Soul, your authentic body of light. Follow the images and symbols in each dream to a learn deeper wisdom of your purpose and journey in this world. You are so much more than you appear to be, keep exploring and discovering more of who you are.

♥Discover the power within you by tuning into your Soul. Everything you deserve is in the palm of your hand and inside your heart. Tonight as you sleep let your dreams lead the way to your hearts content and let your passion surround you like a misty fragrance of possibilities. Your Soul always knows so listen to the wisdom of your Soul and follow... you will arrive where you deserve to be.

♥Dream time is waiting to take you away into the depths of your consciousness beyond the realms of this world. Drift away and delve into the mystery and mystical adventures of your creative imagination deeper than and beyond your passion. Sleep the night away while your Soul travels and explores amazing journey's all while your body rests and restores itself. It's a magical process and you are a magical being.

♥Invite the grace, gratitude and transformation of divine presence to surround you while you traverse the many worlds within your consciousness. Consume the sweetness of Spirit in every way you can and ride this energy of sacred loving into the core of your being and awaken your inner wisdom. Breathe in gratitude and exhale joy, for the blessings already are! From this state of renewal and reverence your passion will be restored.

♥Surrender to the night, let it engulf you and swallow you whole. Float gently into your sleep and weave into your dreams to create the tapestry of your life riding on the wings of your passion within the inner realms. Each thread of your dream carries a vibration of inspiration and majesty of what you may become in your evolution.

♥Envelop yourself in the rapture of nature and release it all to embrace this blessing. Neutrality is the state you will set yourself free! Be present with the gift of "NOW" and launch your Spirit to explore the dimensions of the sacred world of dreams and mystery schools of knowledge. Set sail to explore the inner realms of worlds without end and relish in the wonder and awe of what is possible for you to become, what was written in your heart before you were born.

♥Re-Member yourself to this esoteric level of consciousness as you weave your dreams into this physical reality in your awakened state. Reconnect the fragments through the pieces of your dreams and integrate everything into your being. Let your imagination sparkle with wonder as your dreams lead the way to new discoveries and heightened passions. Have an "ah-ha" night of sweet dreams as you illuminate your consciousness and realign your purpose.

♥Clear the static in your channel, focus on what delights your Soul, connect with Spirit and breathe into your being. As we shift our consciousness to one of authentic peaceful loving and compassion we become a seed for Heaven on Earth. Sleep in peace and know that you are divine, that you matter and that you have a purpose for being here. Ask the sacred light to bathe you and caress you healthy. Let your Soul travel all night long dancing through each dream you have.

♥When you take the time to truly count your blessings I'm sure they'll be more plenty than you previously realized. Gratitude of what you already have been blessed with is a way of being in "blessing consciousness." Bless yourself with an attitude of gratitude and flood yourself with joy for it will stimulate your passion and renew your awareness. Relax and swim into your stream of dreams as you anoint yourself with sacred light.

"Learn to get in touch with the silence within yourself and know that everything in this life has a purpose. There are no mistakes, no coincidences. All events are blessings given to us to learn from." ~**Elizabeth Kubler-Ross**

Judith Ternyik

Creating & Manifesting

You may have created a vision board, an ideal scene and even affirmations which is a good start to program something new in your life. Yet, without actually having it materialize it will remain on paper or in your imagination. Creating is such a positive energetic and nature is creating all around us all the time. When you create it's as if you are collecting the ingredients for the recipe to make what you intend.

Manifesting is actually having your creation come to life and be complete. Taking your imagination and vision boards right into the "here it is" so you can touch, feel and know it has been manifested. These dream blessings will assist you in following through with every intention you have from creation to manifestation. Pay close attention to the clues your dreams show you about this process, how you may be thwarting yourself or ways in which you can engage to guarantee your success.

"Every moment of your life is infinitely creative and the universe is endlessly bountiful. Just put forth a clear enough request, and everything your heart truly desires must come to you."
~Shakti Gawain

♥Dance tonight through all your dreams and tip toe on the colors of light as your Soul travels to new vistas. Your body will rest and heal while your energetic essence engages in new discoveries. Renew yourself with every breath and sink deeper into that place of all knowing. This is the seat of creation this is where you make your dreams come true.

♥Enjoy a sleep of peaceful rest and vivid dreams tonight. Plant the seeds for your next adventure for there is wisdom in the night and magic in your dreams. Breathe deeply as you visualize your clear intention to create and manifest what you deserve to enjoy in this life …now program your dreams to show you the way!

♥Sweetly the night takes us away…. sleep deeply and let your body relax completely. Follow your dreams through the veil into and beyond what you mind can conceive. Let your loving heart lead the way tonight into the places so full of possibility for you to simply acknowledge. Observe and partake in the journey of your Soul travel so you may transform into what you deserve to become. Follow your dreams and live with completion and satisfaction.

♥How will you water your dreams tonight? Energy goes where thoughts & actions go! GO TOWARDS what you deserve to enjoy…. make every night count towards that! Gently breathe and affirm what you want to create as you relax into your sleep and let your dreams take you away. Enjoy precious dreams of joyful bliss moving towards what you deserve to enjoy in lieu of fearing what you want to avoid. Dreams are the gateway to the core of your creativity so dream the night away.

♥Go explore… there is so much more. Good night, sweet blessings to you and yours; wrap yourself in the Light of spirit like a gentle breeze of silk and focus on manifesting your desires. Inhale the intoxicating scent of sweet dreams and explore the mystical magic within each symbol and thought you have tonight. Activate your creative imagination with each dream to clarify what you want to attract into your life now… let the magic begin.

♥Let the day go with gratitude. Acknowledge yourself for wins today. As you fall asleep consider the part of you that is unlimited, eternal, powerful and vibrant. Invite that part of you to lead you into the night of healing rest and bountiful dreams. Count your blessings and know how rich you truly are. Open to the possibilities of becoming greater than you have ever imagined.... for you are limitless. Follow your creative imagination into your dreams so you can manifest the life you desire.

♥Program your Universal Mind tonight with a declaration that your DREAMS will pave the way for you. Heal and balance everything in your life with a prayer and an intention, see and feel what you deserve to receive. Sleep deep, travel with your body of light to new discoveries and realms of wonder. Awaken on all levels and keep seeds of your experience for the new day ahead.

♥Blessings of balance and peace to all tonight, sleep well. Seed your dreams in your fertile imagination and infuse them with the light of Spirit tonight as your body rests. Let your imagination go wild with discovery as you traverse the inner realms of dreams. Plant the seeds of creation and nurture their growth within each dream which takes you closer to manifesting what you deserve to enjoy in your life now.

♥Abundant blessings to you all tonight as you rest, sleep and dream the night away. Share your gratitude for someone, a situation or something that fills your heart with joy. Express your appreciation for yourself, something you did, initiated a new action or just staying present. Ask for answers, direction and awareness in your dreams. Believe you are worthy and deserving of receiving! Allow your dreams to reveal to you your next step.

♥Let's all Soul travel tonight together in loving harmony... nourishing our Soul and connecting with Spirit, as our body rests and our mind creates. May we all bring back a little piece of peace to contribute to our life and our world making a positive transformation for all. Life seems like discovering little bits of the puzzle and weaving it all into our tapestry that is our unique expression. It's time to manifest our dreams come true.

♥Shower your mind with clean thoughts of positive energy as you prepare for a wonderful restful sleep tonight. Bless your physical body by sending healing loving energy to any pain or discomfort so it can be at ease. Fall backwards in your consciousness to a deep sleep as you release your Soul to Travel though the dream realms and beyond. Ask for what you deserve to receive and enjoy then let the universe respond... listen and see beyond your ears and eyes. Awaken in the morning renewed and refreshed with the memories of your night travel with keys to fulfill your life.

♥Image IN "imagine" what you deserve to receive, enjoy and experience. Allow your rest at night and the phases of your dreams to prepare the new you for the new you! Use your creative imagination to "program" the Universal Mind with images of what you want to attract to your life. Ask your dreams to work it out, process it and leave you clues in the morning. Rest assured that your dreams are on your side always supporting you.

♥Set your focus for what you'd like to receive from your dream travel, the answers you seek, the direction or clarity you'd like... and let that focus become your pathway. Open your awareness as you learn and experience altered states of consciousness during your night travels in your body of light, the purity of your Soul, the true essence of who you really are. Dream each dream to completion.

♥Close your eyes and see the darkness until you see the colors of the light. Take a deep breath of peaceful relaxation to prepare for your dream vision. Just observe each dream, image and symbol... they are all keys to unlock the esoteric aspects of you. Allow the vibrant colors you see in your night journey to infuse your being with seeds of creativity and open more discoveries for your awakening consciousness.

♥Open yourself tonight, as you prepare for sleep, to the generous possibilities that are available to you. Surrender your need to know and trust your intuition... allow your process to unfold with splendor. Feel, heal and reveal all that you deserve to experience which will add to your greatness and expand your joy. So very much is available to you. BREATHE DEEPLY...and trust your process. Follow your light into delight. Grace your Soul with the goodness which is at hand. The time is now to manifest your dreams.

♥Surrender your "shoulds" tonight as you slip into your dream state and sleep the night away. Be with the present experience that unfolds for you. Abandon all "set" perceptions to open yourself to the endless possibilities of what may manifest. Become aware of the divine essence that you already are... tune into the vibrational sound and light of Spirit which you also are. "Know thyself" more and more as each night unveils the truth to your consciousness. Each morning, awaken to the knowing of how magnificent and glorious you truly are. With this awareness you are unstoppable in creating anything you desire.

♥Tonight, as you prepare for sleep, let your feelings and thoughts stir and cook for a while until your feelings and thoughts evaporate into thin air leaving you open, peaceful and calm. From this pure empty space create your night journey with the most magnificent dreams. Bathe in the travels and mystical adventures through the vastness of space and time as your Soul gains more awareness. Relax, remember, recharge yourself and be ready to manifest all that you deserve to have.

♥It's time... let this day go... let your past go... surrender it all now. Engage in your sleep, your rest and restoration as you invite a healing balance to begin. Slip into your dream state, the altered state of consciousness where everything you think you know is challenged. Be open to the presence of LIGHT, Spirit and the mystical methods of your dreams which are all available for your enlightenment and transformation. Let go! Let's go, it's time to create!

♥As you close your eyes to prepare for sleep, then open your inner eye to travel your Soul journey weaving through your dream threads. Bring healing grace to your body by blessing it and focusing light on all areas which yearn for greater ease and balance. Set free your mind and your heart to soar into higher realms of consciousness tonight and see glimpses of what may come to be. You have a choice with your voice and what you declare to claim. Blessings of loving light and grace shower you with each breath you take and know that you are a powerful creator.

♥Indulge yourself in the creative process tonight as you drift from dream to dream and anoint yourself with the sound and light of Spirit. Transport yourself into your ideal state of being where you can renew, revive and reveal the most authentic essence of peace and perfection. Bathe in the sacred waters of eternal grace and attain lucid awareness to manifest your dream when you're awake.

♥Ascend into your essence of being as you elevate your awareness into your dream consciousness. Lift past your worldly concerns to become keenly aware of the present, where you are free and peaceful. Reach into the mystical wisdom that is available for you within each dream and trust your intuition for that is where you create from. With each dream you awaken even more. As you awaken more you will manifest the energy to create the life and relationships you desire by radiating a frequency to attract precisely that.

♥Bathe your body in sacred light and anoint your body with healing as you breathe deeply of the night and surrender into slumber. Follow the mystical sound and light into your dreams and relax into the "now" to be present with your awakening as each dream unfolds. Your Soul is remembering and in time your mind will catch up so simply relax and breathe as your essence explores more mysteries of the inner realms with each and every dream. Your creativity will lead you into your dreams and your Soul will help you manifest your dreams.

♥Every symbol, dream, experience is for your unfoldment as a process of discovery of deeper levels of your own consciousness. Dive into your dreams with surrender and wonder as you observe and absorb every single detail as you surrender to the creative process of dreaming within dreams. Connect with each aspect to integrate yourself as a "Gestalt" completion and watch the magic appear in your life each day and you will manifest your dream life.

♥Keep opening your awareness and expanding your energy to encompass so more than you can possibly imagine. BREATHE DEEPLY of the sacred light which is as close as your next breath. The more you open the more you release and receive the goodness of divine creativity, abundance and balance for your life here and now. Peace be still. Sleep deeply and dream in Technicolor while you keep expanding!

♥Protect yourself with your own energetic light, like a Soul enveloped in a cocoon. Set an intention to vibrate to your own rhythm and let that radiate outward to the far reaches of the universe. SLEEP, DREAM, HEAL and receive the blessings. As you fill your heart and mind with gratitude you invite peace and healing to yourself to open the creative vortex of magnificent possibilities. Relax into your sleep, let go and let your dreams take you on amazing adventures of mystical awareness.

♥Let your creative imagination lead you into your streams of dreams tonight. With total surrender of what "should be realistic" boldly jettison yourself fully with wonder and freedom into your dreams. Immerse every breath and cell in your body to experience deeper levels of your consciousness as you begin to awaken more and more with each passing night. You'll discover how great you are at creating through your thoughts, words, dreams and actions and easily manifesting them by day!

♥IF you're anxious it's time to JOURNAL and write your thoughts on paper. BREATHE, BREATHE, BREATHE and return to the center of your being often as you release what no longer serves you. Let go of the past. Surrender your conditioning to usher in and embrace the NEW YOU with each dream that floats through your subconscious mind tonight! When you are clear your creative channel will be open for business and you'll manifest every detail.

♥Bathe your body in the purest light tonight as you relax into your sleep, journey into your dream state and into your creative imagination. Breathe in the radiant light and fill your lungs and organs with renewal to extend this life force through every cell in your body. Surrender to the night and enter the abyss of the other realms trusting in your process and riding your dreams into new discoveries. Keep lifting and expanding for you are always unfolding in the process of transformation. Discover the deeper levels of creativity within you so you will manifest all of your dreams.

♥Stand tall in your Spirit as you ascend in your Soul Body tonight. Allow your physical body to sink deeply into your bed, to rest and restore itself as it sleeps deeply through the night. Surrender your mind and emotions to a pure empty state of being... let the day go as you enter the night with a light-heart. Become like the essence of vapor as you continue to lift into altered states of dream consciousness. Extend your awareness far and wide and remember... you go out on a limb to find the fruit... keep going it's all within your reach this is the process of creating. Enjoy your journey. It's ALL FOR you. Embrace it with rapture.

♥Tonight tell your body to rest, heal, renew and sleep a long restful sleep. Tell your Soul to release and travel the night through, catch a dream and transport your consciousness into the deeper realms of YOU into the creative realm. Relax and enjoy the dream-time journey through the vast depths of subtle energies which may reveal a more real world to you than you realize now. LET GO, LET GOD, LET IT BE...beloved, sweet dreams.

♥Lift your Soul up into the light to the highest realms of creation as you lay down to sleep through the night. Let your dreams be the magic carpet that transports your awareness into and through worlds without end. Remember the fragments and pieces of your dreams that will seed the possibilities for your tomorrows. Heal yourself with the vibration of sound and the radiant light as you journey through this very night. Break free tonight to usher you into manifesting the life you deserve.

"We are such stuff as dreams are made on, and our little life is rounded with a sleep."
~William Shakespeare, The Tempest

Loss & Grief

Filling the empty space of loss is often very challenging especially when we are alone with ourselves trying to get a restful sleep. Coming to terms with the grief and sadness that we feel to the core of our being can take our breath away in fear and panic. Whether it's a loss of a job, finances, a home, a pet, a loving family member or a friend; Loss and Grief can be gut wrenching feelings that leave us lost, empty and confused.

As we experience that separation and empty place we have the opportunity to place loving empathy, patience and nurturing feelings to fill that void. As we take time each evening to "place a blessing" on ourselves and situations that heave us into a challenging emotional state, we bring healing and balance to ourselves. By honoring our feelings of loss and grief we recognize we care enough to feel and in time, through nurturing ourselves with patience and gentle loving, we can get through the worst of the worst. Bless yourself every night with each blessing and see what a difference a month can make.

"Only people who are capable of loving strongly can also suffer great sorrow, but this same necessity of loving serves to counteract their grief and heals them." ~**Leo Tolstoy**

♥Break free tonight, leave your sorrow behind as you ascend into your dream state. See with new vision and explore the mystical realms until you remember more and more. Escape this world and what you have evolved from to embrace the truth as it is revealed to you in every image, in every way. Breathe deeply and let go it's time to dream.

♥Good reminder… Tonight, consider taking a cleansing shower or soaking bath to WASH AWAY the negativity of the day, rinse away any sad feelings and upset as you prepare your body for a renewal tonight. Invite your inner child to cuddle up and anoint yourself with loving light. Sleep peacefully, shower your mind with positive gentle thoughts, fill your heart with goodness and love and be patient with your process as you fill the void with loving light tonight. Your dreams will soothe you and heal you so follow them gently into your sleep.

♥Acknowledge your tender emotions and let your tears anoint you with peace. Prepare yourself tonight for a gentle deep sleep and invite your dreams to soothe your heart. Shower your body to wash the day away, clear your emotions and mind with visions of what can be. Switch the channel to the peaceful dreams channel and renew yourself. Heal your mind, your heart, your body and all of you as you journey into the night with your body of light and return in the morning refreshed, restored new you.

♥You are showered with divine blessings tonight with the sweetest gentle light and sound of Spirit. Breathe in the goodness and let go of your thoughts and feelings and this day as you relax and receive a restful sleep. Sink deeply into your dreams and float on the essence of tenderness, vulnerability and wonder as you bless and discover new vistas within yourself. Listen to your body, listen to your heart, listen to your Soul as all have so much to tell you for you are the blessing and you are the light.

♥Every resonance has a vibration and a harmonic... we are all living on the threads of light in the web of existence interconnected, related and intertwined with all that is. Leave your body behind and soar into your body of light. Separation is an illusion ...we are all... each other in the cosmic eye. Lay to rest all the rest and float into your dreams with an awakening and an intention as you listen to the sacred sound whispering to you "it's ok, you're ok, now sleep."

♥What do you carry in your heart? Perhaps it's time for "spring cleaning" and renew yourself from the inside out. Make each day a new day A NEW YOU! The burdens and sorrow we've carried too long has come to an end. Forgive everything and everyone so you can GIVE to yourself and from that place of renewal give to humanity from a full loving heart. Ask your dreams to paint a new canvas of your new life starting with your next breath.

♥Sweet nocturnal blessings of healing rest for your body, mind and spirit tonight. Allow your human self to drift away into a deep slumber while you awaken to your Soul and experience your Spiritual Light. Engage, Explore, Discover and enjoy the gifts being present will render. RE-member who you truly are... become the blessing you seek. Each dream will offer you a clue to your next steps so keep your dreams flowing so you can keep growing and loving it all.

♥Beloved, fill surround and protect yourself tonight with the Holy Light. Place your prayers in the LIGHT for the highest good for all concerned, and let all concerns fall away. Breathe in the grace and blessings and heal yourself on all levels. Ask and you shall receive. Request that the angels be with you throughout the night. Release your sorrow and your fears to embrace the abundance and fulfillment waiting for you as your dreams lead the way through the darkness into the light.

♥Together we ask for the LIGHT to fill, surround and protect all those who are hurting, fearful and alone. This prayer includes all people and animals alike. Take time to nurture your Soul and soothe your heart, remember that we are not alone, we have the source within us to access and "ask" so we can receive. Let's all open to receive the blessings of loving compassion so we can make a positive difference in our world. Good night to all, sweet dreams for all loving, caring & sharing for all of God's creation.

♥Embrace yourself in the highest vibration of Spiritual Light that you know as your next breath, feeling and thought. Ask for balance, to replace your grief with comfort and your sorrow with loving. Release the day and journey into the vivid realms of colorful light and sacred sound as you sleep the night away and receive a blessing with each dream. Dream sweetly and completely and bring back enough memory in the morning to guide you to your own banquet table of life.

♥Fall into the light of Spirit tonight as you fall asleep tonight. Release your pain, surrender your suffering, let it all go. Transform yourself with each deep breath and renew every cell in your body with divine alignment. Stretch your awareness far beyond your physical body and limitations. Become endless with the essence of who you in all that splendor. You are a sacred thread of God, honor that and expand your loving and anoint yourself with comfort. Invite your dreams to resolve and heal your emotions so you can sleep peacefully.

♥Prepare for a healing sleep... increase your light vibrations so pure that your pain is melted and transformed... shine your light so brightly the dark disappears and the shadows fade. YOU are the LIGHT ...so shine through all that is holding you back, keeping you from your dream life, getting in the way of your connection with Spirit. SHINE ON... DREAM ON... HEAL COMPLETELY... transformation and comfort is at hand, your hands!

♥Ascend this level... let the day go... BREATHE beyond your body and connect with your essence. Lift into higher realms, gain more altitude to perceive everything differently. Spread your wings of consciousness to ride the energy and breath of Spirit into and through your dreams into other vistas of alternate reality. Keep lifting, keep going, keep growing... it's never done. You are a Soul who evolves every second... BREATHE deeply and caress yourself with the light that you are. Let your dreams guide the way and know that this physical world is a temporary place.

♥Sink deeply into your bed tonight, feel your body weight and let it sink deeper. Lift your body of light upward and ascend this world through your dream voyages. Soul Travel beyond the confines of this physical level and delve into mysterious spaces and places that will enrich and nourish your Soul. Let your dreams expand your awareness to encompass all that you are, all that is you which is so much more than your physical form. Become formless in your awakening to bask in the freedom that is present; which is the real gift.

♥Explore the fascinating unique adventures of your night travels within each dream. Relax your body completely so it fully rests and restores while you Soul Travel in your body of energetic light... and make this night a pure delight! Breathe in the depth of awareness as you gently drift into uncharted places within your consciousness. Be embraced by the divine light, let it soothe the hurt and fear and fill you with warmth and loving into and through each dream you have.

♥Nurture your process and embrace the night with fertile dreams as your consciousness branches out reaching further than before. Liberate your Soul to travel throughout the sacred realms as you weave your dream threads together. The deeper you ground yourself and anchor to this world the more freedom you will have to expand into the esoteric realms ascending into greater levels of divine light.

♥Breathe deeply and fully to relax your body as you let go of this physical realm tonight. Release your thoughts and your emotions completely until you're empty. Sink into the recesses of your mind to sleep and restore yourself. Reach out by reaching inward to your authentic consciousness and meet your Soul. Make the connection through your dream travels and expanded consciousness THEN relax even more. Open your heart and shower yourself with loving then extend that energy of loving beyond your body, your home, your country ...and shower all that exists... with your loving while you dream sweetly.

♥It's time to put your thoughts and emotions at rest while your body sleeps and restores. Detach as you surrender this day to the magic of the night you'll prepare yourself for a dream journey while your Soul travels in the light and sound of this divine realm. Take notice, listen gently and be transformed by expanding your awareness to the divine vibrations within your Soul as you dream each dream.

♥Peace is present... just be still and listen for the sound of peace. This worldly level can be so very challenging perhaps a reminder that it a temporary place for us all. Remind yourself that our physical world is but an illusion. Bring your awareness into the light of your spirit until you touch the essence of your Soul. Breathe deeply and fully from that sacred center as you begin your night journey of dream travels with each breath. Be soothed and nurtured with each dream.

♥Lay your body down, allow your sorrow to dissolve and give up this day to give into the night for a healing restful sleep. Let your dreams lure you away from this world into the worlds without end as you traverse inwardly through the canals of light and sound. Keep raising your awareness and lift higher into the gentle embrace of your Soul and indulge in the essence of Spirit. Acknowledge the sacred divine being that you already are and relish in this peaceful state of being.

♥Relax, Sleep, Dream... surrender yourself completely to invite your inner awareness to begin. Dive into the silence of darkness until you see the light and feel the vibration of sound in vivid color surround you. The more open you are the more you will be shown so relax, let go, and go further than ever before into the depths of your dreams. Re-Member yourself to this esoteric level of consciousness as you weave your dreams into this physical reality in your awakened state. Reconnect the fragments through the pieces of your dreams and integrate everything into your being. Be comforted by knowing that whatever is lost will be replaced with greater loving and abundance.

♥Center yourself deep within yourself and let everything fall away that is of this world. Breathe in the sacred breath and move into your pool of peace within your own Soul. Know that you are never alone and beware of the illusions this world presents. Lift into your essence and melt into your dreams as you leave your body behind to rest and heal. As the water ripples outward allow your consciousness to expand into the void until you resonate with the divine light which embraces you always. Others will join to greet you and when you awaken your loss and grief will be replaced with comfort and ease.

♥Detach yourself from the things of this world so you can free yourself to rise above it and enter into the myriad of worlds within your Spirit. Lift past your concerns, sorrows and longing as you stop doing so you can spend time being while you fall asleep and soothe your Soul. Transport yourself through your dreams into the inner realms of mystical light and sound and be greeted with loving joy and reverence. The more you engage in your dreams the thinner the veil will become between here and there the more you will gain Soul awareness and transcend this physical level.

♥Let all that you love and value, envelop you in a cocoon of light tonight. Delve into the mysterious void through the misty fog into your dreamland. As you Soul travel through your dreams your heart will be filled and nurtured with expansive loving light which will lift you above what you are suffering from. Enjoy your dream gems and the mystical wisdom revealed. Let your loving heart rise above and seed greater joy to connect with others from that level.

♥As you prepare for a healing restful sleep, declutter yourself by removing all the layers that you identify as you... release your ego, your name, what you do in this world and all you relate to on this level... strip it all away to acknowledge the core essence of YOU. Stand in the clarity of who you truly are. Now enter the esoteric vapor into your dream world and slip into an altered state of consciousness as the subtle nuances are revealed to you within each dream and symbol. Breathe deeply of your authentic self and trust your process of awakening. Your sorrow and grief will transform into love.

♥Beloved, leave your fears, tears, sorrow, loss and pain behind as you launch your Soul into your dreams tonight. While your body of light traverses the inner realms of mystical wonder your body and mind will stay behind to heal and rejuvenate and balance on all levels while you sleep. You are never alone... feelings are temporary, so let go of the struggle and sleep deeply while your dreams come alive tonight.

♥There is magic in the night and within each dream that presents to you... so embrace your sleep with gentle ease... let the day fade away and tune into your dreams. Love yourself enough to let all your thoughts and feelings go... thank your body and let it sleep. Within each dream you will get a glimpse of a symbol that has a message for you. Be open to unravel the message over time while you patiently enjoy your journey to understanding the meaning of your dreams.

♥Quiet your mind and calm your emotions to invite your body to release, relax and heal. LISTEN to the silence and hear the drum, strum, sound and vibration that is speaking to you ...like a "sound current" with sacred messages of wisdom for your Soul. Dreams are portals which we travel without our physical bodies... when we release and relax enough we open ourselves to receive greater gifts then we can even imagine.

♥Hush the sounds outside of you so you can listen to the sound within. Bless your body with thanks and healing thoughts as you begin your night journey into slumber. LISTEN to the distant subtle sounds of the "sound current" which may appear as light and images at first. Let your dreams transport you to sacred realms of mystery and wisdom beyond what your mind may understand. Shhh, listen, sleep and dream the night through for dreaming is balancing and healing to your Soul and your heart will again rejoice.

♥Quiet yourself by calming your feelings and closing off your thoughts so you can allow a peaceful state of being to emerge from within. Breathe deeply to inhale the calm nectar of the night and let it permeate every cell in your body to induce a healing soothing process. Meander into the ethers of light and sound to begin your dream journey with wonder and grace. Let your Soul be your guide as you traverse the peaceful realms of light weaving through your dreams with freedom and wonder. You are free... peace is present.

♥Let your body become heavy and sink deeper into your bed, into the floor and anchor itself deeply into the Earth to be grounded, cuddled, comforted and healed. Elevate your awareness towards your Soul body as it ascends into the night, into your dreams. Be transformed by the divine light and sound you will encounter traveling through your dream saga. BREATHE DEEPLY of this sacred peace and be still as you receive what is perfectly manifested just for you. You are loved and protected always AND in all ways.

"Father, O father! What do we here...In this land of unbelief and fear? The Land of Dreams is better far, Above the light of the morning star." ~**William Blake, "The Land of Dreams"**

Transformation & Change

It's been said that "change is hard" but consider that remaining the same may actually become harder! Without change it's probable that we may eventually feel stuck. When we continue on with the same old, same old, it's easy to fall into a predictable life and become complacent. Living in a constant state of tolerating and compromising what is less than ideal may set up a frustrating life to live. Where would butterflies be if caterpillars never wrapped themselves up in a cocoon?

Changes occur in our life when we move and relocate, change jobs or careers, change life partners, gain new friends and sometimes experience life altering circumstances. The key to change is transformation. As we transform we are able to embrace the change more gracefully. These dream blessings will support you in opening to the possibility that you are constantly being transformed on some level every day. It's in the transformation that we are made new again, reborn in a way and see through a new set of eyes as we gain a more lucid understanding. Set your dreams free to show you the path to transformation.

"Personal transformation can and does have global effects. As we go, so goes the world, for the world is us. The revolution that will save the world is ultimately a personal one." ~**Marianne Williamson**

♥The ability to place your dreams above your fears will determine the quality of your life. Transformation is a process so relax into your sleep and allow the process of change to unfold. Dream sweetly tonight and return with keys to build your dreams during the daytime too! Dream deeply and fully as you pay attention to what to remember.

♥Yes, "go within" and refocus your energies. This process, whether you call it Meditation, Visualization, Athletes Zone, Mental Imagery or whatever. IT IS A PEACEFUL PROCESS OF SELF EMPOWERMENT. Some cultures may connect with God, Spirit, Divine light (whatever else you may call it) Others may simply focus on the physical and psychological bodies for healing, balancing, clearing and so on. Clear, center, prepare yourself for a night of revealing dreams for change is at hand.

♥Seek your core and find the divine thread of Spirit to strum your way into your dreams tonight. Vibrate with the sound of sacred perfection and follow your streaming consciousness deeper into the dream realm to discover more of what is available to you. Bathe your body in light, breathe deeply of the sacred breath and transform yourself on every level. Give yourself permission to reveal and remember your dream gems for that will be your foundation of transformation.

♥Tonight as you drift into a deep sleep to restful healing sleep, invite your Soul to expand and soar into other realms of existence. Learn to see without your eyes and hear without your ears. There are so many depths and layers of who you are than you may realize. All you have to do is to surrender and explore what's possible for you to discover. Become limitless and expansive as you ride the energy of loving discovery to who you are for change is how we evolve.

♥Change is at hand and with each breath relax deeper into your peaceful calm. Allow every second wash away the day, your anxiety, your past. Drift into another consciousness and reality of dreams, Soul travel with Spirit throughout the night. Delight in the blessings bestowed upon you in every way for tomorrow is your day, a new happy you, embrace it all as you accept the transformation you yearn for.

♥Each night before sleep, bless yourself, our world, all people, nations, animals, plants and simply ALL OF GOD'S CREATION. Through change we create life. Send out loving light in radiant streams to flow and touch all with a blessing of loving comfort, peace and ease during this time of change. As you drift into your dreams release any karma and recall tomorrow what you can take forward into a new day. This process will invite the change you deserve and to live in a transformed world that we all pray for.

♥Dream-time beckons you to journey deep within during this time of change and transformation, into the worlds without end. Fill yourself with so much light and vibration that you lift from your body, into and through the ethers of consciousness to a mystical and sacred place. Let the light and sound heal you while your Soul soars beyond your imagination. Rest and restore while your dreams reveal deep wisdom. Sleep well and dream sweetly and transform with grace.

♥We're all in the PROCESS of TRANSFORMATION. Life is a process not an event. TRUST your PROCESS and KEEP EVOLVING... just keep going no matter how slow or small. It's the CONSTANT and CONSISTENT actions that will transport us to all that we deserve! Release your dreams and imagination tonight and journey into magical realms.

♥Fall asleep into the darkness tonight and soothe your body and mind with rest. Let your inner light shine the way through layers of awareness as your Soul travels into other dimensions. Bring your light into the darkness of human consciousness; and let's all contribute to transforming humanity into greater compassion, loving and caring for all creation. You already are "the light," so keep illuminating every moment like a constant mantra of loving truth. Transform yourself and you'll transform our world.

♥Let your body in its form, rest and sink deeply into a healing slumber. Allow your Soul to expand into the formless wonder of realities beyond. Seek and explore the authentic you that you already are. Return to integrate all that you can remember and plant new seeds tomorrow for a better you and a better world. Multi-dimensional awareness is a great asset to have and utilize, keep expanding into the wisdom available.

♥Restore yourself tonight with the light from your Soul and the light from Spirit. Shine through the dark pathways into your vivid dreams and learn about the possibilities waiting for you. Fill, surround and protect yourself with the most Holy of LIGHT and release what which no longer serves you as you embrace the new experiences into your life. Ask, declare and receive for it is the transformation that keeps us evolving.

♥We are the authors of our own dream, the artists of our creation and the choreographers of our life. We can REVISE and UPDATE our dreams each and every night, it's the way to seed the change you desire in your life while you're awake. Then allow the subconscious to develop it while we sleep! Shall we edit and update our dreams tonight, while our body rests, our Soul travels? Let our dreams transform us into greater focus and conscious awareness!

♥Leave the roller coaster of life behind tonight... lift your awareness beyond your body to float along the stars and become lighter than air. Your physical body will self-heal; simply bless it and move towards your Soul Travel tonight. Each dream clears the way for your consciousness to expand like the galaxies themselves. Take in the light, the brilliance, the colors and transform with the process. Engage all that you are aware of... all that is you as you know it. Keep evolving for there is so much more. Let the loving presence embrace you throughout the night and relish in your sweetest of dreams.

♥Peacefully sleep and profoundly heal tonight as you dream deeply to discover more of you which is always in a constant state of transformation. Awaken with a greater degree of enlightenment and radiate your LIGHT into all that you do. Transform your life a second at a time, a cell at a time, a blink at a time ...dig deeper and reach higher. YOU are waiting for YOU.

♥Surrender your body to your bed as you sleep and lift past this level through your dream zone to enter the mystical and magical realms of light and sound. Witness the display of light and images with wonder and purity in lieu of thinking of meaning and purpose. Just be present, open to change and give yourself that gift of being in the now. When your consciousness is open and expanded much will be revealed to you. Dream sweetly, dream deeply, dream the whole night through as you awaken with each dream and transform your life a night at a time.

♥Sleep deeply as you ascend fully into your dream dimensions. Be alert as you transcend this physical level into the finer subtle levels of mystical light and essence. Bathe in this sacred light and anoint yourself in the Holy presence of the one who travels with you on your journey within the inner realms. Open, ask, receive and breathe deeply of the Divine blessings present for you within your dreams. Keep evolving, changing and transform into the more authentic you.

♥Change is an evolution... our cells change in our body every day; our bones renew in months, your whole body in one year. YOU are always CHANGING and challenges are a way of nudging your feelings and thoughts to change also to MATCH THE NEW YOU! Dream of what may become and seed that vision! Dreams are just the beginning!

♥Cradle yourself in the arms of the Beloved tonight as you release the day and prepare for sleep. You are filled, surrounded and protected with divine light and the soft whispers of angels around you. Embrace change and breathe deeply of the peace which is present each moment for you. Float gently into your world of dreams. Open your heart to receive all the gifts that await your claim. Partake in the mystical magic of your dreams in the night and cherish the gifts that are being bestowed upon you.

♥Wake up in your dreams tonight into a place that soothes your Soul and transforms you on every level. Breathe deeply of the sacred breath, and invite that pure light to bathe you into resilient health. Release your mind and emotions completely and surrender all that you think you know, to open yourself to the greater more that awaits your acknowledgement. Tune into the sound current and ride that energy into the heart of all being. Vibrate with greater balance, and joy with each breath. Awaken to the possibilities present for you as you make your dreams come true.

♥Receive deeply of your next breath and sustain it through your body as you exhale let everything leave your body that is not in balance with divine perfection. Take in a gentle breath and invite your dreams to usher in and take you into the deeper levels of your being. Transform yourself into every possibility which will seed to your health, wealth and harmony, by delving deeply into each dream. The more open you are and less attached to what should be; the more gifts you can receive though the magic of the night.

♥Transform yourself as you ascend into your dream vortex into and through the inner worlds without end. Return to the light of which you already are and traverse the dream realms as the brilliant light that you are. Transform and transcend with each breath and connect with the purity of essence that you are being already…which is: LIGHT.

♥Gently float away into your dreams within wisps of light as you glide on the ether of Spirit. Be enlightened with the mystical majesty of these inner realms of worlds without end. Surrender all that you know to simply be present and accept the changes occurring. Receive the wisdom available to you, and transform your life into myriad miracles. Now rest, sleep and renew the best is yet to come so prepare to receive.

♥Breathe in deep relaxation so your body will rest, restore and heal while your inner light extends its wings to soar into your dream realm. Transform into the essence of who you are and permeate the layers between here and there. Sift through your dream images into greater knowledge from the pools of wisdom beyond this world. Continue to transmute anything that is less than divine perfection in your process of awakening and the changes coming to you. Dream sweetly all night long and awaken in the morning graced with blessings.

♥Lay down, stretch your body out to begin your relaxation and transformational dreams. Breathe in the peaceful silence and cuddle up with the dark of night. Let your mind ponder and drift along the dream waves of light. Escape this world as you Soul travel into worlds without end. Gather the wisdom and keys to transcend and transform as you dream the night away. Change is the process of life itself, so celebrate!

♥Open your heart so it overflows with loving like lava to drench you with compassion and sweetness over your body and into your Soul. Surrender your attachments and concerns of this world so you can ascend into the brilliant light where the nectar is intoxicating with divine rapture. Drift into your dream tunnel and be transformed on many levels. Embrace this night and the process of change with joyful delight and relish in the loving.

♥Breathe deeply and expand your lungs completely then expand your body fully, and as you release that breath, let everything totally empty from your thoughts and feelings. Breathe gently as you send light to your physical body and settle down for a long restful sleep. Feel the vibration of light tingle on your skin, as you transform into the essence of energy and melt into your dreams. Observe your dreams and gather the gems of wisdom for you to remember long after the dream is over. Awake each morning a "new you," with more dream gems to apply to your life for the changes you deserve to have.

♥Elevate your awareness towards the "you" beyond your physical form. Breathe deeply and relax your body so you can ascend this level within each dream into the consciousness of your higher self. Keep moving upward where there are no words, just sound and light. Then partake of this sacred awakening within your being. Your dreams may serve as a portal or gateway towards connecting to your divine source. So relax, embrace the change, breathe and dream the night away as you illuminate your Soul.

♥Dissolve yourself; your ego, personality, thoughts and feelings tonight and breathe in calm, peace and illumination. Peacefully drift into your dreams and trust your process of unfoldment for change is good. Honor yourself by allowing your dreams to lead the way and build your foundation of trust each night. Tune into a transformational night of dreams.

♥Prepare the canvas of your imagination for the healing empowering dreams that will transform your life... renew yourself now by putting this day far away. Plant a seed in your consciousness with a dream intention of change and relax your body into your sleep. Now... let go and follow your Soul into your dreamy night as you trust your process and receive the blessings of changes that will transform you.

♥Stretch your body to relax and rest, stretch your mind and emotions until they are calm. Stretch your imagination into the ethers of light as you drift through the veil of dreams. Let every sound, vibration and ray of light permeate every cell towards change, renewal and awakening. The more you awaken the more you'll know and the more you know the further you'll go. Remaining the same is not the game so change, shift and transform now!

♥Take in a long deep breath and sustain your inhale as long as you can... fill yourself with life and feel the changes in your body. Release your breath fully to attain a more relaxed state as you prepare for a transformational sleep tonight. Dance on the thread of your being and follow the energy that you are into the colorful dimensions within your dreams. Be light and free as you allow this energy move you towards greater awareness and blessings that await your awakening.

"Even while the Earth sleeps, we travel." ~**Kahlil Gibran**

Nightly Blessings of Sacred Prayer

Beloved Father-Mother God,

Please open our hearts and our minds to align with our Souls so that we all will become a blessing for each other and our Mother Earth.

Infuse us with your divine light so we may radiate health, peace and restoration to every living creature on this planet, so that each one of us carries the seed of transformation, change, love, peace and harmony.

May we all begin to vibrate with one accord to the divine sound and light of God and heal ourselves and our planet... let this be so... sweet dreams.

Baruch Bashan (the blessings already are)

Rev. Judi Ternyik

About the author

Judi is a Transformational Coach empowering people to integrate and balance their lives while living their dreams. She is an inspirational speaker, motivational leader and enjoys "provoking lives" to make a positive impact in the world.

Throughout her 40 plus year career in gymnastics as a coach, judge, consultant and speaker, Judi has developed a system using "Body Psychology" to educate others about health, wellness and peak performance in her work with Body Smarts Coaching.

Judi is passionate about mentoring children and adults, athletes and executives in the art of effective communication, self actualization, self esteem and team dynamics. "When we are whole and complete we are able to successfully pursue our endeavors with greater consistency and ease."

When we learn now to heal the pain, both physically and psychologically, we are better able to cope with our daily routine and gain momentum to create the life we deserve to enjoy.

Judi also designs and facilitates educational workshops, seminars and retreats which center around self development, team building and personal growth. Judi has presented a myriad of topics to small and large groups and also works with clients via Skype and phone sessions. She has a You Tube channel, Vlogs and Blogs which offer entertaining thoughts, provoking topics and suggestions on how to live more fully with passion and purpose.

To hire Judi for speaking presentations and group or private coaching sessions:

Please contact Judi at: www.provokeyourlife.com or JudgeJudi@JudiTernyik.com

Judi's next book, due to be published in 2017, is about "Body Psychology" which is the foundation of Body Smarts Coaching.

Made in the USA
Middletown, DE
12 September 2016